TOOLS

FOR

IGNITING

CURIOSITY

TOOLS
FOR
IGNITING
CURIOSITY

Classroom-Ready Techniques for Increasing Engagement and Inspiring the Love of Learning

Over 20 tools for

- Sparking curiosity
- Sustaining curiosity over time
- Cultivating curious, self-motivated learners

Bryan Goodwin | Harvey F. Silver | Susan Kreisman | Matthew J. Perini

Silver Strong & Associates
Thoughtful Education Press

McREL
INTERNATIONAL

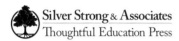

3 Tice Road, Suite 2
Franklin Lakes, NJ 07417
Phone: 800-962-4432 or 201-652-1155
Fax: 201-652-1127
Website: www.ThoughtfulClassroom.com
Email: questions@thoughtfulclassroom.com

President and Tools Series Developer: Harvey F. Silver
Director of Publishing and Tools Series Editor: Matthew J. Perini
Project Manager: Matthew J. Perini
Design and Production Directors: Bethann Carbone & Michael Heil
Proofreader: Rachel Rosolina

4601 DTC Boulevard, Suite 500
Denver, CO 80237-2596
Phone: 800-858-6830 or 303-337-0990

Website: www.mcrel.org
Email: info@mcrel.org

CEO and President: Bryan Goodwin
Chief Marketing & Innovation Officer: Ron Miletta

A number of tools featured in this book have been adapted from other titles in the Tools for Today's Educators series, including *Tools for Classroom Instruction That Works* (A Study In…; Anticipation Guide; Before, During, After (BDA); Mystery; Window Notes), *Tools for Thoughtful Assessment* (What Comes to Mind?; From Puzzles to Paradoxes), *Tools for a Successful School Year* (Forced Choice), and *Tools for Conquering the Common Core* (Claim Check).

All web links in this book are correct as of the publication date below but may have become inactive or otherwise modified since that time. If you notice a deactivated or changed link, please email questions@thoughtfulclassroom.com with the words "Link Update" in the subject line. In your message, please specify the web link, the book title, and the page number on which the link appears.

Printed in the United States of America

Quantity discounts are available. For information, call 800-962-4432.

ISBN: 978-1-58284-218-9

Library of Congress Control Number: 2019951761

25 24 23 22 21 20 19   1 2 3 4 5 6 7 8 9 10

Acknowledgments

Because so many people helped make this book possible, the question is, Where to start? We think the obvious place to start is with Abigail Boutz. A longtime member of the Tools for Today's Educators team, Abigail's insistence that every tool meets the highest standard is the greatest quality control a writing team could hope for.

We also owe a debt of gratitude to Justin Gilbert, for effortlessly managing so many critical editorial and production tasks; Kimberly Nunez, for coordinating with the educators who field-tested new tools; Edward Thomas, for being our math sounding board and advisor; and Joyce Jackson, for keeping us focused on the needs of young learners.

In addition, we want to thank the many educators who have made the tools in this book better by testing them in their classrooms and schools. Two schools in particular have been wonderful learning labs and action research partners. The first school we'd like to acknowledge is Children's Aid College Prep Charter School in Bronx, NY, with a special note of appreciation for principals Casey Vier and Robin Fleshman and teachers Elizabeth Pena, Alexis Vilceus, Daequan Lawrence, and Isaac Fosu. The second learning lab school we want to recognize is Millennium Community School in Columbus, OH, with particular thanks to Executive Director Tijuana Russell and teachers Nicole Anloague and Krystal Coulter.

Finally, we want to thank these thoughtful educators who both inspired and helped us throughout the process: Brett Fickes of Thornton Township High School District 205 in South Holland, IL; Stephen Sturgill of Sandusky City Schools in Sandusky, OH; Anne Blankenship of Westbrooke Village Elementary School in Trotwood, OH; Nicholas DiSanto of Affinity Schools, New York City Department of Education; and Lisa Granieri and the teachers and administrators from the West Babylon School District, NY, who have supported the discussion of our tools on their Reflective Pathway blog.

For copies of the reproducibles
and other downloadable extras noted in the text,
visit **www.ThoughtfulClassroom.com/Tools**.

Contents

Foreword

During my youth, I lived on a small dairy farm in upstate New York. Not far from our house was a small creek that flowed around a curve. While paving the roads, the county decided that this curve, which had been there for who knows how many years, needed to be straightened. In came the workers with their heavy equipment, digging, filling, and ignoring completely the natural bend of the creek. My father, a cornucopia of folksy sayings, warned them repeatedly: "You can't go against Mother Nature." Of course, they disregarded him, as the job had to be done.

What do you think happened?

With the very first heavy spring rain, the road washed out completely. So the county went to it again, this time bringing in the really big machines, extra gravel, and steel reinforcements. And sure enough, the next spring's rains washed the road out a second time. On the third try, the county got the bright idea to incorporate the natural flow of the creek into their design. Today, decades later, the road remains, curving in unison with the creek.

As so often turns out to be the case, the truth is simple, and my father was right: Going against nature is a fool's errand.

Unfortunately, I hear my father's words echoing in my mind with alarming frequency in my work as an educator. Why? Because it seems that far too many schools seem to have forgotten that children are curious by nature: Young children seek what or who is hiding behind the curtain; they yearn to discover what's inside an unopened package; they wonder why the sky is blue. Regardless of ethnicity, socioeconomic background, or family conditions, you'll see the same glimmer in the eyes at that moment of discovery, when a student can say with pride, "Ah-ha! I figured that out, and now I know."

This natural curiosity doesn't end in grade school. Children, adults, *humans* are inherently curious. When confronted with almost anything new, humans immediately get to wondering: What is *this* and what am I in relationship to it? And yet, even though this curiosity is natural and naturally motivating at any age, our schools often fail to capitalize on and cultivate it. Perhaps it's the concern over test scores or the pressure to cover the content that has gotten us to this place. Whatever the reason, our response should be the same: We need to design and deliver instruction that goes with the natural flow of students' curiosity.

So here's the good news: Going with the flow of students' curiosity doesn't need to be difficult. And better yet, when teachers and schools commit themselves to teaching with curiosity in mind, things change dramatically.

I have seen this great power of curiosity make a difference at every level.

I remember so clearly from my days as a young teacher what that glow in twenty-five children's faces looked like when they finally solved a mystery I had set up for them. That look gave me the energy to do even better the next day.

As a gifted coordinator and a principal, I worked with teachers to design instruction with the thread of curiosity running through every lesson and unit. So often, parents would come to my office to express their gratitude, overflowing with excitement because their child was looking forward to coming to school for the first time since kindergarten.

And today, as a consultant and coach to schools around the country, I see both the presence and the lack of curiosity on an almost daily basis. What I can tell you from this work is that every single school that makes a point of nourishing students' curiosity sees the same outcomes: higher levels of engagement, deeper understanding, and most important, a love of learning that you can feel when you walk down the halls and enter classrooms.

That's why I am so excited about this book. It shows educators how to go with the natural flow of students' curiosity to raise excitement, enhance learning, and help students hone their curiosity into a powerful learning mindset. The book takes the best research on curiosity and provides user-friendly tools that help teachers put the research to work in ways that will enliven and enrich any classroom, starting tomorrow.

The tools work. I have helped educators around the country integrate these tools into their practice, and the results are always striking. "Teaching is fun again," so many teachers say. And of course, that fun is infectious, influencing students and their attitudes toward learning. One teacher recently told me that the high level of excitement she now sees in her students "almost makes her cry." This is what happens when educators have real tools for putting curiosity at the center of their work. The entire culture changes into a "home for the mind"—a place that inspires the love of learning.

So, let's use these tools to inspire that love of learning in our students.

Let's go with the flow.

R. Thomas Dewing, EdD
Education consultant and author

Welcome to "Tools for Today's Educators"

The book you are holding is part of Tools for Today's Educators, a series that we began publishing more than a decade ago. We began creating tools—classroom-ready techniques for improving teaching and learning—because the teachers we worked with were asking us for simple but effective solutions for problems they faced in their classrooms. They wanted practical techniques for addressing these problems, not theoretical ones; techniques that they could implement quickly, without a lot of advance planning; and techniques that could be adapted for use in different grade levels and content areas. Most of all, they wanted techniques that would work in real classrooms with real students.

Over the years, we have kept these requests in mind as we developed the various books in our Tools line. We have also continued to ask teachers about the challenges they face in their classrooms, so that we can provide them with tools for addressing those challenges.

This particular book was inspired by an almost universal longing that we hear teachers express all the time: How can I create that energy—that spark—that will get students genuinely excited about learning? To help answer this question, we turned to Bryan Goodwin, a great educator with a simple but powerful message: Curiosity, the most natural of learning drives, is the key to igniting teaching and learning.

For some time now, Bryan has been using his voice to show how classrooms, how schools, how students' futures change dramatically and for the better when educators make curiosity a guiding principle. We are excited to have collaborated with Bryan to develop this set of ready-to-use tools, which helps teachers put the best research on curiosity into everyday classroom practice. This joint publication between Silver Strong & Associates and McREL International is one that we are confident will help you rekindle your passion for teaching and inspire a lifelong love of learning in your students.

Please let us know how the tools are working for you and your students. We would love to hear from you!

Harvey F. Silver
Series Developer

Matthew J. Perini
Series Editor

Introduction

Yearning for Learning

We're all born with curiosity, that innate "yearning for learning" that helps us make discoveries about the world around us. And that's a good thing because curiosity, as you'll see, is pretty powerful stuff.

Put aside the ancient "curiosity killed the cat" adage warning us about the dangers of inquisitiveness. Curiosity—and more specifically, teaching with students' curiosity in mind—is one of the best ways to engage students in deep learning. When students are curious, they're more motivated and goal directed as learners (Kashdan & Steger, 2007), and they're more likely to retain what they've learned (Gruber, Gelman, & Ranganath, 2014). Perhaps most important, when students are curious, they *enjoy* learning. Brain research shows that satisfying our curiosity activates the dopamine reward centers in our brains, creating an urge to "scratch that itch" by learning more (Aron, Shohamy, Clark, Myers, Gluck, & Poldrack, 2004). With this in mind, it's not surprising that studies have found that curiosity is as strongly linked to student performance as persistence, attentiveness, and even IQ (Shah, Weeks, Richards, & Kaciroti, 2018; von Stumm, Hell, & Chamorro-Premuzic, 2011).

But the benefits of curiosity go well beyond the classroom. Curiosity is a key to a richer, more fulfilling life. Indeed, research also tells us that people who approach the world with an abiding curiosity tend to do better in their careers (Reio & Wiswell, 2000), demonstrate better leadership skills (Fernández-Aráoz, 2014), experience higher levels of satisfaction (Kashdan & Steger, 2007), and live longer lives (Swan & Carmelli, 1996).

Perhaps the best news of all for teachers is that curiosity isn't some new theory, nor is it a "movement of the moment" that educators sometimes feel beset by. Curiosity is a universal feature of being human, as evidenced by the enthusiastic questioning and exploring we all do as toddlers and through our first few years of school—Why do my parents kiss (yuck!)? What happens to all those poor fish when the pond freezes? How can an airplane fly through the air? Why do people speak different languages? What will happen when Harry Potter and Voldemort finally face off?

However, this faucet of questions that young children turn on so readily will not necessarily remain turned on forever. If we don't nurture our curiosity, or if we find ourselves in environments that suppress curiosity, it will diminish. And sadly, studies have found that the longer students stay in school, the more their curiosity wanes (Engel, 2011; Engelhard & Monsaas, 1988; Gottfried, Fleming, & Gottfried, 2001). If you're an upper elementary, middle, or high school teacher, you've probably seen students who've become more reluctant to ask questions, more unwilling to take on academic challenges, less interested in wondering what new learning lies beyond today's lesson.

In *Out of Curiosity* (2018), one of the authors of this book, Bryan Goodwin, made a case from research for why we need more curiosity in our lives and our schools. *Out of Curiosity* asked us to imagine what might be possible in society if we could "unleash the deep kind of curiosity that lies at the heart of discovery, science, and enlightenment, and serves as the lifeblood of democracy" (p. x). So let's get curious about *that* for a moment. What would happen if we created that yearning for learning in our classrooms and schools every day? Wouldn't teaching and learning be a bit—and maybe even a lot— more joyful? And wouldn't that joy lead to better results? And to more interested, more interesting, and ultimately more successful students?

How to Get the Yearning for Learning Burning

We can hear you saying, *Yes! But how? Specifically in my classroom tomorrow, how do I use curiosity to capture students' interest? How do I sustain curiosity long enough to deepen students' understanding of a topic? How do I help my students see the world through curious eyes?*

It is that string of questions and, more particularly, those three little letters—*H-O-W?*—that led us to write this book. This book answers the question of *how* by providing over twenty practical, research-based tools that you can use to put the power of curiosity to work in your classroom. Both the design of this book and its tools are deeply informed by the work of Bryan Goodwin and his colleagues at McREL International, who have conducted a deep analysis of the research on curiosity and the best practices for promoting it in schools (Goodwin, 2018; Goodwin, Gibson, Lewis, & Rouleau, 2018; Goodwin, Rouleau, & Lewis, 2018). The book's three-chapter structure and corresponding tools provide everything you'll need to kindle the flame of curiosity in your classroom and ignite the kind of "intellectual fire" that drives and motivates deep learning.

- In Chapter 1, Sparking Students' Curiosity, you'll find tools you can use to start the fire, or get students interested in and excited about new learning.

- In Chapter 2, Fanning the Flame of Curiosity, you'll find tools that will help you keep the fire of curiosity burning, or sustain students' interest and engagement over the course of lessons and units.

- In Chapter 3, Creating an Inner Fire, you'll find tools designed to stoke students' "fire inside," or inspire students to pursue their own natural curiosity.

The question of what tools to include in each chapter ignited an intellectual fire in us. We worked together to select, modify, and, in many cases, develop all-new tools that would help teachers "get the yearning for learning burning" in their classrooms. These tools are drawn from the work of Harvey Silver, Richard Strong, Matthew Perini, and Abigail Boutz, who have created and refined hundreds of ready-to-use instructional techniques for enhancing teaching and learning (Boutz, Silver, Jackson, & Perini, 2012; Silver, Abla, Boutz, & Perini, 2018; Silver & Boutz, 2015; Silver, Perini, & Boutz, 2016; Silver, Strong, & Perini, 2001).

Tools for Igniting Curiosity is the result of this collaborative effort: a collection of research-based, classroom-ready tools that you can use to spark curiosity, keep it burning, and turn it into something more—a self-sustaining inner fire that will motivate your students to pursue new learning for the rest of their lives.

Key Design Features of This Book

To help you understand what the book contains and how to use it effectively, we've summarized some of its key design features in the sections that follow.

Designed to work for busy teachers

We know how busy teachers are, and we structured this book accordingly.

We kept things short and simple, so that tools could be put into practice quickly. A description of each tool, its benefits, and steps for implementing it can all be found on a single page. Most tools require little or no advance planning, and all have seven or fewer steps.

We formatted each tool so that critical information would be easy to find and use. Every tool contains the same four basic sections (see figure below). Large, boldface headings let you jump to whichever sections you're interested in and in whatever order works best for you.

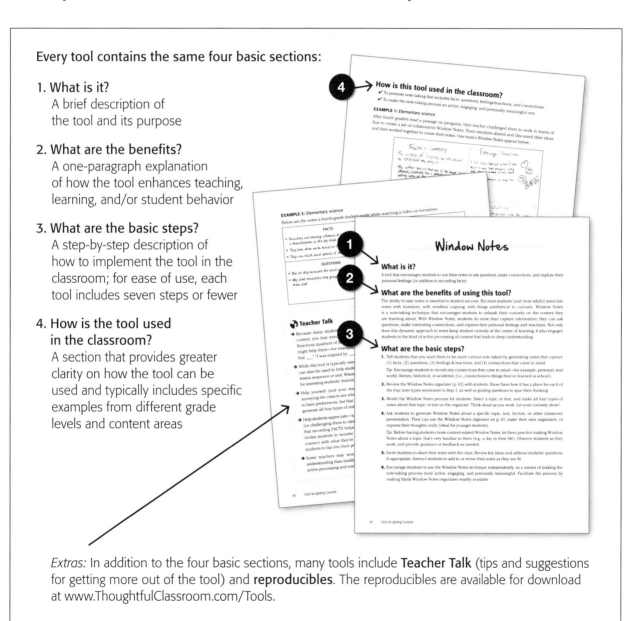

Every tool contains the same four basic sections:

1. **What is it?**
   A brief description of the tool and its purpose

2. **What are the benefits?**
   A one-paragraph explanation of how the tool enhances teaching, learning, and/or student behavior

3. **What are the basic steps?**
   A step-by-step description of how to implement the tool in the classroom; for ease of use, each tool includes seven steps or fewer

4. **How is the tool used in the classroom?**
   A section that provides greater clarity on how the tool can be used and typically includes specific examples from different grade levels and content areas

Extras: In addition to the four basic sections, many tools include **Teacher Talk** (tips and suggestions for getting more out of the tool) and **reproducibles**. The reproducibles are available for download at www.ThoughtfulClassroom.com/Tools.

We provided everything you need to get the tools going in your classroom. Besides the essentials, such as easy-to-follow steps and ready-to-go reproducibles (available both in the book and on the book's companion website, www.ThoughtfulClassroom.com/Tools), many tools include Teacher Talk, a bonus section that includes tips from practitioners, implementation suggestions, and other useful information. Skimming these Teacher Talk sections before trying a tool for the first time can help you avoid potential pitfalls and start using the tool like an expert.

We designed the book to be easily searchable, so you don't have to read it from cover to cover. Skim the one-sentence "What is it?" descriptions to find a tool that meets your needs, or use one of the book's search features:

- Use the Table of Contents (p. vii) to find tools that will help you address each of the three goals for promoting curiosity in the classroom (sparking curiosity, fanning the flame, creating an inner fire).

- Use the chapter introductions (pp. 9–10, 35–36, and 63–64) to get a quick, thumbnail description of each tool, so you can decide which tools are right for you and your students.

- Use the Index of Tools (p. 97) to search for tools by name.

Designed to work in real classrooms

The tools in this book are aligned with current research on how best to capture and harness student curiosity. More than that, though, they're designed to work in real classrooms with real students. To get the tools working in your classroom, be sure to review them thoroughly (including classroom examples and teacher tips), modify them as needed, and use them regularly. Stop after each use to reflect on how things went and steps you might take to make the tool work even better the next time you use it.

To facilitate this kind of reflection, we've included a simple reflection form and guidelines for creating a reflection journal in the Epilogue (pp. 91–92). Whenever possible, engage in the reflective process with your colleagues, so that you can learn from each other's experiences and offer each other suggestions ("The way I simplified this tool to make it work for my kindergarteners was . . .").

Designed to be used across grade levels and content areas

All teachers can benefit from integrating curiosity into their everyday practice. This book shows you how to get the curiosity fire burning in your classroom by including a variety of examples that reflect a range of grade levels and content areas. Use the examples and Teacher Talk tips to see how tools can be adapted to meet specific content and classroom demands.

Designed to be used with colleagues

Creating a curiosity-driven classroom takes commitment. The good news is that you don't have to make this commitment alone. Because this book can be used across grade levels and content areas, you and your colleagues can support each other as you learn, practice, and refine your use of individual tools. Present a tool at your next staff development meeting and make a schoolwide effort to implement it. Commit to trying a new tool on a regular basis with your professional learning community (PLC). Or, do what a group of educators in West Babylon, New York, did and create a blog where teachers can share and learn from each other's experiences with specific tools (http://reflectivepathway.blogspot.com).

Committing to learning tools with your colleagues will help you implement the tools more confidently and promote student curiosity more effectively. Think, for example, how much better students will be at asking questions and pursuing learning goals based on their own curiosity if those are skills that your whole school has been focusing on. And consider how much richer the conversations will be among staff members if every teacher is using a common set of tools to develop these behaviors and skills from the earliest grades on up.

Designed to be used by administrators as well as teachers

The tools in this book aren't just designed to help teachers; they're designed to help administrators grow their capacities as instructional leaders. Principals and other school leaders can use the tools to provide teachers with concrete suggestions for targeting and improving specific elements of their classroom practice. This process is beneficial when used with individual teachers ("During my observation, I noticed that some students seemed a bit disengaged, even though you were passionate about the content. Using the Mystery tool to turn your next content-heavy lesson into a mystery that students have to solve might help with this") or as part of a schoolwide initiative to target particular curiosity goals ("Many staff members are working to improve their lesson openings to spark student interest right from the outset. Over the next month, let's all commit to using at least two tools from Chapter 1 to help us get more out of our lesson-openers"). Note that focusing on specific tools schoolwide is a great way to get everyone on the same page and ensure that classroom goals are aligned with school goals.

Designed to enhance any school improvement initiative

No matter what your school's priorities or improvement goals are for this year, next year, or for the long term, curiosity is a natural fit that will always make your work better. In other words, don't think of curiosity as one more thing to add to a list of priorities; think of how it can help make what you're already focused on better. For example, if it's project-based learning that's driving your improvement goals, keep in mind that students are far more likely to commit to producing high-quality work if we align that work with their interests and curiosity. Or, if your school or district is focused on social and emotional learning, consider this: Helping students exhibit genuine curiosity about the lives and experiences of others can serve as an "antidote to loneliness, detachment, and declining empathy in our world" (Goodwin, 2018, p. 91). Or maybe your school's goal for this year is to finally become a true professional learning community. If so, don't forget about curiosity. Why? Because your efforts will go so much further if team members are encouraged to wrestle with problems of practice and pursue solutions that matter to them. It's amazing what a little curiosity can do, but it should come as no surprise. After all, curiosity creates a passion to learn, and any improvement effort will work better when it's driven by passion.

Designed to help you and your students establish a curiosity mindset

With our help, curious students will become curious adults, and curious adults, as we have discussed, live more successful and more satisfying lives than incurious adults. Thus, we need to treat curiosity not as something we sometimes think about to enhance lessons, but as something we embody, something we inspire in our students every day. Use the three broad chapter goals of this book as a guide whenever you design and deliver instruction: How will I capture students' attention? How will I keep students actively engaged in the learning? How can I invite students' own curiosity into the lesson or unit? Select the tools that will best help you achieve these goals in relation to your content. And show students how the tools work by modeling them in the classroom before asking students to use them on their own. These moves can help you turn your classroom into a curiosity training camp—a place where students can practice and develop their curiosity skills until they become second nature.

· · ·

Perhaps the simplest definition of curiosity is the desire to learn more. Thus, teaching with curiosity in mind needs to be a goal of every teacher because every teacher is in the business of developing lifelong learners. And as lofty and challenging as that goal may sometimes seem, what if it's actually quite simple? What if all we need to do is prioritize curiosity and let the tools in this book do the work? We know these tools work because we have seen their impact in classrooms across the country. We have seen roomfuls of first graders who can't wait to use the Forced Choice tool (pp. 24–27) to make the case about whether insects are more helpful or more harmful to humans. We have seen the Questions Are QUESTS tool (pp. 55–57) transform the act of learning across an entire middle school— to the point that students pose their own questions based on their own curiosity and then go out on self-directed learning quests to look for answers. And we have seen how a tool like 13 Ways of Looking at a Topic (pp. 11–14) can inspire teachers to fall in love with their content all over again so that their students have the chance to fall in love with that same content for the first time. In all of these cases, it's the gleam of curiosity that we're seeing, and it's a gleam that changes minds, that creates that all-important yearning for learning, potentially for the rest of our students' lives.

So what about you? Are you feeling this yearning for learning? We certainly hope so as we hand these tools for igniting curiosity over to you.

Sparking Students' Curiosity

You can't start a fire without a spark.

—Bruce Springsteen

People who are curious learn more than people who are not, and people learn more when they are curious than when they are not.

—Susan Engel, *The Hungry Mind: The Origins of Curiosity in Childhood*

Curiosity is the key to turning learning into its own reward, a self-replenishing source of enthusiasm for discovery and knowledge. But it has to start somewhere. Just like a roaring fire begins with a small spark, curiosity begins with an initial wondering—a question prompted by recognizing that you don't know it all and that filling in those gaps in your knowledge can be not only beneficial, but also downright exciting.

Clearly then, we need to find ways to spark that initial moment of curiosity and help students realize that things might be a bit more interesting if they knew more— even if just a little more—about the topic at hand. What happens next? Where's the missing piece? How does it work? Whodunnit? Why do people care about it? How is it relevant to my life?

This chapter is about that initial spark—and increasing your commitment to creating that spark so that students get excited about the learning in your classroom. It's about how to push, pull, and prod young minds so that they embark on the learning journey eager to know more. But it is also about the residual effects of making such a commitment. Indeed, the more you make a point of piquing students' curiosity, the more you'll help students see that *being curious is fun* and that when they're curious, the fun never ends. That's because every answer leads to a new question—a new gap in knowledge to close, a new mystery to solve, a new puzzle to piece together, a new intellectual horizon to chase.

Of course, it takes a curious mind to fully appreciate just how exhilarating this never-ending quest to learn can be. And cultivating such curious minds, which is the ultimate goal of this book, must have a beginning. That's where the tools in this chapter come in.

In this chapter, we present seven tools to help spark students' curiosity:

1. **13 Ways of Looking at a Topic** shows teachers how to find the most interesting elements of the topics they teach—and how to capitalize on those elements to boost student curiosity.

2. **A Study In . . .** helps teachers frame lessons and units around universal concepts that provoke thinking and invite deep exploration of content.

3. **Anticipation Guide** sparks curiosity by challenging students to take positions on classroom content before learning and encouraging them to revisit their positions after learning.

4. **Curiosity Catalysts** shows teachers how to design captivating lesson starters ("hooks") using five research-based conditions that stimulate the desire to learn.

5. **Forced Choice** provides teachers with simple frames that capture students' attention and increase engagement with classroom content by creating "controversy in an instant."

6. **Think of a Time** uses the power of personal experience to enhance curiosity and deepen understanding of important subject matter.

7. **What Comes to Mind?** is a quick and easy way to unlock students' background knowledge and use that knowledge to increase interest in the learning to come.

13 Ways of Looking at a Topic

What is it?

A planning tool that uses a set of simple questions to help teachers find the aspects of a topic that will foster student curiosity and energize teaching and learning

What are the benefits of using this tool?

Have you ever considered just how incredible a volcano, or the Pythagorean Theorem, or the Bill of Rights really are? Classroom content is truly full of wonders. Sometimes, though, teachers are so close to their content that they can forget how rich and amazing it can be. When this happens, teaching can go flat, quashing student curiosity. This lesson-planning tool, which is inspired by Wallace Stevens's famous poem, "Thirteen Ways of Looking at a Blackbird," is designed to help teachers rekindle (or kindle for the first time) their love affair with the content they teach. It provides thirteen distinct ways of searching for curiosity-boosting "best bets"—those aspects or attributes of classroom topics that excite teachers' passion to teach and spark students' desire to learn. The tool also helps teachers integrate these best bets into their lessons and units.

What are the basic steps?

1. Select a topic that you are about to teach.

2. Review your own understanding of the topic. Identify the big ideas and key supporting details that you want students to understand.

3. Use the questions at the top of the 13 Ways Planning Form (p. 14) to help you find particular aspects or attributes of the topic that are especially interesting to you and/or likely to spark student curiosity. Check off any ways that you plan to pursue in your lesson or unit.

   Note: The goal isn't to check off all thirteen boxes. Instead, look for a manageable number of best bets that you believe have the greatest chance of raising curiosity in relation to the topic.

4. Decide how you will integrate your chosen best bets into your lesson or unit. Use the space on the 13 Ways Planning Form to work through your ideas. Here are some questions you might ask about each best bet to help you integrate it into your instructional design:

   • Can you build a lesson around it?

   • Can you design a task around it?

   • Can you conduct a discussion or Socratic Seminar on it?

   • Can you connect it to students' lives, experiences, and concerns?

   • Can you create an essential question to help students explore it deeply?

   • Can you engage students in an inquiry into its causes and/or effects?

How is this tool used in the classroom?

✔ To find the aspects of a topic that are most likely to raise student curiosity

✔ To facilitate lesson and unit planning that will increase students' desire to learn

✔ To energize teaching and learning

EXAMPLE 1: Primary science

In planning an extended lesson, a first-grade teacher decides to use just one question from the 13 Ways Planning Form ("What's amazing about it?") to open students' eyes to the wonders of something they take for granted—trees. To begin the lesson, she places a large poster at the front of the room with the question "What's so amazing about trees?" During the extended lesson, the teacher regularly stops, redirects students' attention to the poster, and captures any new and "amazing" information that the class has learned about trees. The completed poster is shown below.

EXAMPLE 2: Secondary ELA

A high school English teacher is planning a unit on Shakespeare's *Othello*. He uses the 13 Ways Planning Form to look for new ways to increase student curiosity in the play. Below are the four ways the teacher settled on as best bets, along with his notes for how to integrate each best bet into the unit.

Othello

What's UNIQUE about it?

- Iago = evil genius

- He is considered one of the greatest villains ever created.

- What's so uniquely disturbing about him is that he uses people's goodness against them: "So will I turn her virtue into pitch, / And out of her own goodness make the net / That shall enmesh them all."

How to integrate: Iago is an archetype and the model for several pop culture villains who adopt his tactics. I will challenge students to find examples of pop culture villains based on Iago and explain their choices.

What's CONTROVERSIAL about it?

- Depictions of race and gender

- Is it racist?

- Is it sexist?

- Is it fair to judge works of art by today's standards?

How to integrate: These questions will make for a rich and provocative Socratic Seminar. I will encourage students to take on the controversy directly during the Socratic Seminar.

What's RELATABLE about it?

- Jealousy

- Love

- Manipulation/gullibility

- Passions getting the best of us

How to integrate: These are universal themes and emotions we've all experienced. Throughout the unit, we will regularly discuss connections to students' own lives. Students will write in their journals about their feelings, reactions, and relevant experiences.

What good is it in the "REAL WORLD"?

- How can a play written over 400 years ago help us learn how to manage our emotions?

How to integrate: This will be one of the essential questions for the unit. We'll use it to look at ourselves and to explore the idea of "Shakespeare the psychologist"—someone with preternatural insight into human behavior.

---

13 Ways Planning Form

Which ways of looking at your topic are your "best bets" for sparking student curiosity?

☐ 1. What's unique/novel/unprecedented about it?

☐ 2. What's controversial about it?

☐ 3. What's strange/mysterious about it?

☐ 4. What's relatable about it?

☐ 5. What's humorous/funny about it?

☐ 6. What's amazing / hard to believe about it?

☐ 7. Why do people care about it?

☐ 8. What's something about it that most people overlook / don't know / get wrong?

☐ 9. How do people react to it? What are some different perspectives or opinions on it?

☐ 10. What good is it in the "real world"?

☐ 11. Where are there opportunities within it to create suspense?

☐ 12. Where are there opportunities within it for students to make discoveries?

☐ 13. What about it gets you fired up? Why are you excited to teach it?

How will you incorporate your best bets into your lesson or unit?

A Study In...

What is it?

A simple technique for framing instructional units around core concepts that focus student learning, provoke student thinking, and promote deep exploration of important ideas

What are the benefits of using this tool?

Any good instructional unit should be designed around clear learning targets. But if our goal is to help student curiosity flourish, then clear targets are not enough; each unit should also be what Art Costa (2008) calls "a home for the mind"—a place that encourages deep thinking and inquiry. One way to build this curiosity-conducive quality into our units is to frame them around core concepts or universal themes. This tool shows teachers how to design their units around the biggest of the big ideas—that conceptual powerhouse that puts all of the other concepts into line. With a rich concept guiding their learning, students are better able to explore the content, make connections, and develop new insights.

What are the basic steps?

1. Identify the key understandings that you expect students to develop over the course of a unit.

2. Ask yourself, "What core concept or universal theme unites these key understandings and can serve as a lens for investigating the content of this unit?" For a list of universal concepts that provoke deep thinking, see Teacher Talk.

3. Turn your concept into a unit title using this format: "Unit Topic: A Study in Core Concept."

   Note: You are not simply restating the topic of your unit, so think conceptually rather than literally. A conceptual title such as "The Water Cycle: A Study in Renewal" will provoke student thinking about the importance of water far more than "The Water Cycle: A Study in Precipitation."

4. Use the core concept to promote deep learning throughout the unit. Some ways to do this include

   - *Using the concept as a hook for the unit.* Introduce the title of the unit, and invite students to think about what they know about the topic and the core concept.

   - *Designing essential questions around the concept.* Have students explore the concept deeply using essential questions. See Teacher Talk for more on the relationship between core concepts and essential questions.

   - *Developing a culminating assessment around the concept.* For example, a unit titled "The Water Cycle: A Study in Renewal" might culminate with a task that asks students, "What can the water cycle teach us about nature's power to renew itself?"

   - *Encouraging regular reflection.* Come back to the concept throughout the unit. Ask students to think about how their understanding of the concept is growing.

   - *Building interdisciplinary thinking.* Teachers can work together to build units that highlight common concepts. For example, how might a concept like *design* play out in three different units, one focused on literature, one focused on art, and one focused on STEM?

How is this tool used in the classroom?

✔ To use rich, universal concepts to promote curiosity and deep learning

✔ To develop students' ability to think conceptually

✔ To increase students' interest in academic topics

Teachers at all grade levels use this tool to frame their units around thought-provoking concepts. Below are some examples of unit titles developed with this tool.

• *Frog and Toad*: A Study in Friendship

• The Four Seasons: A Study in Change

• The Energy Crisis: A Study in Responsibility

• Equations: A Study in Balance

• The Civil Rights Movement: A Study in Courage

• *The Grapes of Wrath*: A Study in the American Dream (or Nightmare?)

• Four Films by Hitchcock: A Study in Obsession

🌓 Teacher Talk

➔ Are you looking for some universal concepts that dependably lead to robust thinking? Try these:

Adaptation	Creativity	Patterns
Balance	Design	Perception
Caring	Discovery	Perspective
Cause and effect	Ethics	Prejudice
Change	Friendship	Relationships
Community	Inequality	Renewal
Competition	Interdependence	Representation
Composition	Interpretation	Revolution
Conflict	Needs and wants	Structure and function
Convergence	Order	Supply and demand
Courage	Organization	Survival
Craftsmanship	Parts and wholes	Systems

➔ In *Teaching for Deeper Learning*, Jay McTighe and Harvey Silver (2020) show how to adapt this tool so that the students, rather than their teachers, "identify broad concepts and themes that can unite, focus, and illuminate the content they're learning" (p. 19). To use the tool in this student-driven way, ask students to review their learning about a topic and to search for (or select from a teacher-provided list) a broad concept or theme that ties the content together. Invite students to share their choices and support them with evidence by providing a "because." For example, "I see the Civil Rights Movement as a study in courage because ...," "I see *Charlotte's Web* as a study in friendship because ..."

➔ The core concept that you derive using this tool can be an ideal basis for developing essential questions for your unit. For example, an ELA team that designed a unit titled "Argument: A Study in Craftsmanship" asked students to explore the following essential question during the unit: What does it mean to craft a convincing argument?

Anticipation Guide

What is it?

A tool used to activate students' prior knowledge, get students to take positions on upcoming topics, and sustain curiosity by challenging students to search for evidence to support their positions

What are the benefits of using this tool?

Agree or disagree: *Money can most definitely buy happiness*. Are you thinking? Chances are good that you are because the simple act of agreeing or disagreeing with a thought-provoking statement stirs the mind to life. Anticipation Guide, which is based on the work of Harold Herber (1970), is a tool that taps directly into this curiosity-boosting power. By providing students with a set of statements about the learning to come, Anticipation Guides activate students' prior knowledge and help students get a pre-learning grasp on the content. By requiring students to take a position on each statement, the tool helps sustain curiosity, as new learning becomes an active search for information that supports students' positions. And by asking students to review the statements after learning and decide anew whether they agree or disagree, Anticipation Guides teach students to reflect on how their thinking has grown or changed.

What are the basic steps?

1. Identify a lesson, unit, reading, video, or other important chunk of content that you want students to understand deeply.

2. Generate a list of statements about the content of the lesson or learning chunk. Statements can be true, false, or open to interpretation/designed to provoke debate.

   Tip: For research-based suggestions on how to write effective statements, as well as tips on how to ensure that your statements pique student curiosity, see Teacher Talk.

3. Ask students to read the statements carefully, make sure they understand them, and decide whether they agree or disagree with each statement. Remind students that they are not expected to have "correct" responses; they should make their best guesses based on what they know.

4. Survey students and probe their responses for the reasoning behind their positions.

   Note: Surveying responses and encouraging students to explain their thinking provides a wealth of pre-assessment data about students' knowledge of the content and reasoning skills.

5. Conduct the lesson. Encourage students to be on the lookout for information that can help them confirm or rethink their positions.

6. Have students review their positions. Ask them if their initial positions have changed or been reinforced. Challenge them to justify their positions using relevant information from the lesson.

7. Use students' responses to evaluate both their understanding of what they've learned and their ability to support a position with evidence.

How is this tool used in the classroom?

✔ To provide students with a curiosity-piquing preview of the learning to come

✔ To encourage students to use their prior knowledge to take positions on new content

✔ To increase engagement in an upcoming lesson

EXAMPLE 1: Elementary science

An elementary teacher is about to begin a unit on insects and wants students to think deeply about what insects are and how insects affect their lives. After a brief introduction, the teacher presents an Anticipation Guide (below) and reviews all of the statements with students. Both before and after the lesson, students decide if they agree or disagree with the statements and explain why.

Before the lesson		Statements	After the lesson	
Agree	Disagree		Agree	Disagree
		Insects are good team players.		
		Life would be better if there were no annoying insects like mosquitoes and ticks.		
		Spiders are insects.		
		Some insects have superpowers.		
		Insects help humans.		

EXAMPLE 2: Secondary history

A high school history teacher teaches an elective called So Much Change, So Little Time: The 1960s through the 1990s. As part of a unit on the sixties, students learn about popular music and how it changed during the decade. Before and after learning about the music of the sixties, students respond to and discuss the statements in the Anticipation Guide below.

Before the lesson		Statements	After the lesson	
Agree	Disagree		Agree	Disagree
		Popular music is a product of its times.		
		Popular artists should avoid taking political positions on controversial issues; their job is to entertain.		
		Music can be a powerful form of protest.		
		Kids from every generation hate their parents' music, and parents hate their kids' music.		
		Today's musicians want nothing to do with old music from previous generations.		

Teacher Talk

➔ What does it take to design effective Anticipation Guide statements? According to Duffelmeyer (1994), well-designed statements meet the following criteria: (1) They preview important ideas that students will encounter, (2) they are general rather than overly specific to the content, (3) they activate and help students draw on relevant prior experiences, and (4) they often draw out misconceptions about the content.

Use the classroom examples on p. 18 to see what these effective-design criteria look like in practice, and keep these criteria in mind when you generate your own statements.

➔ While the Anticipation Guide tool naturally engages curiosity by challenging students to search for information and verify their ideas, you can further enhance student interest by making some of your statements extra "juicy." Here are some tips:

- *Stir up debate.* Write statements that are polarizing, that you are confident will "divide the room" and get students thinking. For example, "Building a wall across our southern border is the most effective way to address illegal immigration."

- *Be blunt.* Sometimes, framing statements in simple, stark language is the quickest way to grab attention and stimulate thinking. For example, "Social media is a complete waste of time."

- *Fire up the emotions.* We often lead with our emotions, so developing statements that can trigger emotional responses is a surefire way to raise interest. For example, a high school English teacher who was about to begin *Romeo and Juliet* presented this statement to her students: "Teenagers are too naive and self-centered to understand what true love really is."

- *Say it in a way that runs contrary to what most students think.* Statements that defy expectations or challenge common assumptions can increase curiosity. For example, to challenge young learners' understanding of birds, a primary teacher used this statement: "Not all birds can fly."

Curiosity Catalysts

What is it?

A set of lesson and unit starters designed around research that identifies the ideal conditions for sparking curiosity

What are the benefits of using this tool?

Many teachers make common practice of beginning their lessons and units with hooks—opening activities that activate students' prior knowledge and preview the learning to come. But how well do these hooks spark curiosity so that students approach the new learning with excitement, with the driving desire to learn more? Curiosity Catalysts identifies five research-based conditions ideal for sparking student curiosity. More important, it shows teachers how to use these five conditions to make their hooks especially intriguing. The tool also reminds teachers to focus the curiosity that a good hook creates by bridging students' ideas to the upcoming learning.

What are the basic steps?

1. Think about the topic and learning goal(s) of an upcoming lesson or unit.

2. Design an engaging question or activity (a "curiosity catalyst") that you can use to introduce the overall topic and/or a specific learning goal. See the numbered list on p. 21 for general ideas; see pp. 21–22 for concrete examples.

   Note: A well-designed curiosity catalyst should capture students' interest, get students thinking about the relevant content, and help students activate prior knowledge.

3. Present your curiosity catalyst at the outset of the lesson or unit. Invite students to think about it and then share their responses.

   Tip: Give students time to think before asking them to respond. To help students deepen their thinking, ask them to write down their initial responses and then have them share with a partner or small group before sharing with the class.

4. Collect and summarize students' responses.

5. Connect the question or activity that students just completed (the curiosity catalyst), along with students' responses, to the content and/or learning goals of the lesson you're about to teach. This bridging move is called the "content connection."

6. Incorporate curiosity catalysts and content connections into your lesson plans as often as possible. To maximize engagement, use different types of curiosity catalysts for different lessons rather than falling back on the same type every time.

How is this tool used in the classroom?

✔ To preview content, activate prior knowledge, and increase curiosity before lessons and units

Teachers of all content areas and grade levels use Curiosity Catalysts to introduce lessons and units in ways that increase students' interest in the learning to come. Drawing on research about what makes learners especially curious (Goodwin, 2018; Loewenstein, 1994), this tool focuses on creating hooks that use five specific conditions shown to "catalyze" curiosity:

1. *Manageable knowledge gaps* boost curiosity because our minds are wired to fill in the perceived "missing pieces" in our knowledge. To create this condition, build hooks that use missing information (e.g., incomplete sequences, unfinished narratives, riddles, puzzles) to draw students in.

2. *Guessing and receiving feedback* capitalizes on the way the natural desire to learn increases after incorrect guesses. To create this condition, design hooks that will elicit incorrect guesses that are rooted in common misconceptions about the content.

3. *Incongruities* tap into the curiosity-piquing power of paradoxical phenomena. To create this condition, open a lesson with a fact, visual, or demonstration that defies expectations or seems counterintuitive.

4. *Controversy*, by its very nature, incites curiosity. To create this condition, encourage students to explore debatable issues and controversies within classroom content.

5. *"Someone knows something we don't"* provokes curiosity by letting students know there is a secret and that they're not in on it—yet. To create this condition, present information that encourages students to make predictions about something that will be revealed later (e.g., the topic of an upcoming unit, the outcome of a story).

The examples that follow show what each of these types of Curiosity Catalysts looks like in the classroom. Each example also shows how the teacher creates a "content connection" that focuses student curiosity where it belongs—on the upcoming learning.

EXAMPLE 1: A Curiosity Catalyst that uses *manageable knowledge gaps*

An American history teacher aimed to spark curiosity at the start of a lesson on the Jamestown Colony by presenting students with a "missing-information puzzle" to solve.

CURIOSITY CATALYST: The men and boys who left London behind and set sail for America in 1606 to establish a British settlement had high hopes for their future. They could not have anticipated the terrible fate that awaited most of them. Within three years of arriving in Jamestown, Virginia, 440 of the original 500 settlers had died. Despite the arrival of new colonists and new supplies, the mortality rate soared to much higher levels than would be expected. What was going on? Why were so many people dying?

CONTENT CONNECTION: Keep your eyes and ears open during today's lesson and see if you can find any clues that will help you solve the puzzle.

EXAMPLE 2: A Curiosity Catalyst that uses *guessing and receiving feedback*

A middle school math teacher knows from experience that students (incorrectly) think that prior events affect subsequent events, even when the events are independent. She thus decides to open a unit on probability with the curiosity catalyst below, which is intentionally designed to elicit incorrect answers based on this common misconception. The idea behind intentionally eliciting incorrect answers is that students become curious to learn the correct answer once they learn that their initial answers are wrong.

CURIOSITY CATALYST: If I told you that I had just flipped this coin ten times in a row and gotten tails every time, what do you think would be the most likely outcome if I flipped it again?

CONTENT CONNECTION: So, a lot of you said *tails* because I seemed to be on some kind of "tails streak"—and a lot of you said *heads* because you thought it wouldn't be possible to continue getting tails. Actually, neither of those answers is correct. Let's see why . . .

EXAMPLE 3: A Curiosity Catalyst that uses *incongruities*

An elementary teacher uses the curiosity catalyst and content connection below to draw students in at the start of a unit on animal behaviors and adaptations.

CURIOSITY CATALYST: Sea otters spend about eleven hours per day sleeping or resting. Given that they sleep in the water, you'd expect them to drift away or get separated from other otters in their group while sleeping—but they don't. How is this possible?

CONTENT CONNECTION: Today we'll explore the answer to this question. We'll also investigate some other interesting animal behaviors and adaptations that I think you'll enjoy learning about.

EXAMPLE 4: A Curiosity Catalyst that uses *controversy*

A US Government teacher aims to spark interest in topics that students don't normally get excited about—in this case, the Electoral College—by posing curiosity-provoking questions that lead students to explore controversies within those topics.

CURIOSITY CATALYST: How is it possible in a democracy that the presidential candidate who wins the most votes doesn't necessarily win the election?

CONTENT CONNECTION: You'll discover the answer in today's lesson. You'll also examine the ongoing controversy over the fairness of such a system—and decide for yourself whether that system should be reformed, left alone, or abolished.

EXAMPLE 5: A Curiosity Catalyst that uses *"someone knows something we don't"*

A primary-grade teacher uses "guess the secret" curiosity catalysts at the start of storytime to get students curious about the books they're about to read.

CURIOSITY CATALYST: In the book we're about to read, a lady swallows a shell, a crab, a fish, a gull, a pail, some sand, and a wave. Why do you think she does that? Does anyone have any guesses?

CONTENT CONNECTION: At the end of the book, the author reveals the answer. Let's read and see whether any of your guesses were correct . . .

🌑 Teacher Talk

→ Here are some questions to help you design and implement high-quality curiosity catalysts:

- What key idea, concept, or information do you want students to understand as a result of your curiosity catalyst?

- Will students have relevant background knowledge or experience to draw on?

- What will you need to do to set up the curiosity catalyst? Will students need a video, visual aid, story, reading, demonstration, or other source of information to make the hook work?

- Is the curiosity catalyst engaging? Will it spark student curiosity?

- What do you expect to hear in students' responses? How will you guide their thinking to broaden their responses?

- How will you summarize students' responses?

- How will you connect students' responses to the learning to come? What particular angle or way in do you want to use for the content connection?

Forced Choice

What is it?

A tool that sparks curiosity and develops argument skills by challenging students to take and defend positions on content-related "controversies"

What are the benefits of using this tool?

When it comes to raising curiosity in the classroom, both research (Lowry & Johnson, 1981) and experience tell us that a little controversy goes a long way. Yet, despite its potential to energize learning, many teachers steer clear of controversy in their classrooms, likely for two main reasons: (1) They sense that controversy isn't particularly applicable in their content area or grade level, and (2) they worry that it can lead to disagreements that ultimately become disruptions. Forced Choice allows all teachers to harness the power of controversy by addressing both of these challenges directly. It gives teachers simple frames that create "controversy in an instant" by forcing students to take and defend a position on whatever they're studying—including content that students don't typically get excited about. It also teaches students how to discuss and debate their ideas respectfully, using evidence and reasoning rather than personal confrontations to make their case.

What are the basic steps?

1. Review the Forced Choice Frames on pp. 26–27. Pick one that appeals to you and fits your content.

2. Use the selected frame to develop a content-specific question or statement that will provoke debate when presented to students. Confirm that your question or statement is one that students can have legitimately different opinions about, not one that has a definitive right or wrong answer.

Note: The goal is to develop questions or statements that pique curiosity and require students to think deeply about the relevant content (review important details, clarify key concepts, etc.).

3. Present your question or statement. Give students time to develop a position and gather evidence. Clarify that there are no right or wrong answers, just different opinions.

4. Prepare students to engage in a heated but respectful discussion by reviewing and modeling the following discussion guidelines (modify the list as needed):

- State your positions clearly. Support them with relevant facts, reasons, and evidence.
- Treat your classmates as you'd want to be treated. If you're going to disagree, do it respectfully.
- Question and critique each other's logic and evidence, not each other's intelligence.
- Be passionate about your positions, but listen to other people's arguments as well.
- Keep an open mind. Feel free to change positions in response to what you hear.

5. Invite students to share and justify their positions. Moderate the discussion by helping students recognize faulty or insufficient evidence, transform personal attacks into thoughtful critiques, etc.

6. Help students reflect on what they learned and how well they followed the discussion guidelines.

How is this tool used in the classroom?

✔ To use controversy and debate as a means of stimulating student curiosity

✔ To promote active conversations about (and a deeper understanding of) critical content

✔ To develop students' ability to support a position with solid reasons and evidence

✔ To develop essential speaking and listening skills

Teachers use the Forced Choice Frames described on pp. 26–27 to engage students in discussing key content and discussing it excitedly. Sample prompts show how the frames can work across grade levels and content areas.

🎯 Teacher Talk

→ Remind students to support their "forced choices" with reasons and evidence by saying, "And you chose that position *because*?" (Students should respond with, "I think ____ because ____.")

→ Forced Choice provides an ideal opportunity to review and give students feedback about their use of behavioral guidelines that relate to sharing and discussing ideas—guidelines like listening carefully, disagreeing respectfully, and critiquing ideas rather than people. As always, remember to teach expected behaviors explicitly, provide reminders as needed, and offer specific and informative praise to students who exhibit the behaviors successfully. ("I appreciate that you questioned Santiago's logic rather than attacking Santiago personally.")

→ Despite its seemingly contentious nature, Forced Choice is actually an ideal tool for teaching students how to compromise. Once students have laid out their arguments, consider asking them whether compromise is possible. ("Can you come up with a position statement that everyone in the class can agree with?") Students who are arguing about the merits of genetically modified foods, for example, might agree to the following compromise: "Genetically modified foods should at least be labeled so consumers can avoid them if they want to."

→ Be sure to leave time for reflection (Step 6). Help students solidify their understanding of the relevant content (and demonstrate they were listening) by challenging them to summarize their classmates' positions and evidence. Prepare students to become more actively and appropriately engaged in future discussions by helping them assess—and think about how to improve—their performance. ("How well did you personally follow our discussion guidelines? How well did the class as a whole follow the guidelines? How can you/we do better next time?")

→ As written, the tool develops oral argument skills, but you can target written argument skills instead by having students present and justify their positions in writing rather than orally.

Six Forced Choice Frames

More Alike or Different?

More Alike or Different? is useful when students are studying related pairs of items, events, concepts, or individuals. To use this frame, have students review what they know about each item, decide whether the items are more alike or different, and support their choices with relevant details. Asking students to decide whether two items are more alike or different and explain their reasoning forces them to examine the items more closely and attend to the most salient similarities and differences. Here are some sample prompts:

- Are reptiles and amphibians more alike or more different?
- Are fractions and decimals more alike or more different?
- Are Jackie Robinson and Billie Jean King more alike or more different?
- Are these two poems more alike or more different?

Help students reflect on and analyze their decision-making process by calling attention to the criteria they use to make their choices. ("John argued that these paintings are more similar than different because their subject matter and color palette are almost identical. What criteria was Tameka using when she decided that the paintings were more different?")

Which Is More ... Better ... the Best ... the Most?

This frame asks students to make and defend judgments based on quality or degree. Prompts contain comparative or superlative words such as *more*, *better*, *best*, *most*, and *greatest*. Here are some examples:

- Which of these articles provides the most useful advice for managing stress?
- Which type of graph is best for presenting this kind of data?
- Which of these inventions had the greatest impact on human history?

Agree or Disagree?

With this frame, students are given debate-provoking statements rather than questions. Students decide whether they agree or disagree with each statement and then justify their decisions with appropriate evidence. Here are some sample statements:

- Children my age should have a set bedtime.
- The United States should adopt the metric system.
- This design plan is better than that one.

This or That?

This frame forces students to make a choice between two opposing characterizations of (or viewpoints on) a specific item, individual, or topic. Prompts take the form of questions like these:

- Is "playground time" useful time or a waste of time?
- Is Holden Caulfield hopelessly naive or wise beyond his years?
- Is nuclear energy more helpful or harmful?
- How should we remember the Age of Exploration—as a time of great discovery or a time of terrible exploitation?

As with all the frames in this tool, students are expected to support their positions with evidence.

Metaphorical Duels

Metaphorical Duels (Silver, Brunsting, Walsh, & Thomas, 2012) exploits the power of metaphorical thinking to promote depth of understanding. To use this frame, design two possible similes around a topic of interest, ask students which they feel is the most accurate, and have them justify their choices. Making the unusual connections that this frame requires forces students to think deeply and creatively about the critical attributes of the initial topic—a move that can have a powerful impact on curiosity and lead to truly insightful revelations. Here are some sample prompts:

- Is a good friend more like a teddy bear or a flower?
- Is prejudice more like an iceberg or a runaway train?
- Is the scientific method more like a recipe or a map?
- Are graphing calculators more like microscopes or telescopes?

Encouraging students to describe the attributes of the items they're comparing can help them make more thoughtful and well-supported choices. ("Before deciding whether prejudice is more like an iceberg or a runaway train, jot down everything you know about prejudice, everything you know about icebergs, and everything you know about runaway trains.")

A Study in Opposites

This technique is adapted from the pioneering work of W. J. J. Gordon (1973) and his use of compressed conflicts. A compressed conflict is a way of drawing out the conceptual tension within topics by describing them using two contradictory terms (e.g., How is Jay Gatsby a *cowardly hero*?). A Study in Opposites adapts this idea by challenging students to choose two opposing terms that they believe shed light on the topic under investigation. Once students choose their terms, they must explain their reasoning. Here are some examples:

- The Renaissance is a study in *revolution* and *tradition* because ...
- Our community is a study in *cooperation* and *competition* because ...
- Probability is a study in *clarity* and *uncertainty* because ...
- I am a study in _____ and _____ because ... [Students choose two contradictory terms that describe their personalities.]

Unlike other Forced Choice frames that provide ready-made options for students to choose from, this frame offers open-ended choice. The ultimate goal is for students to be able to choose, on their own, two opposing terms that reveal something essential about the topic. However, getting students to this point will likely take some scaffolding work. Early on, you might provide the opposing terms directly. Another option is to allow students to select two opposing terms from a word bank or word wall. As students become more familiar with this frame, encourage them to choose their own terms and help them refine their choices as needed. In all cases, students must explain how the two terms help illuminate the topic.

Think of a Time

What is it?

A tool that invites students to examine a concept from three perspectives: when it affected them directly (participant), when it affected others (observer), and when they supported someone who was experiencing it (supporter)

What are the benefits of using this tool?

Simply stated, we increase curiosity in our classrooms when we help students connect what they're learning to their personal experience. Think of a Time (adapted from Brownlie, Close, & Wingren, 1990) is a tool that puts this premise to work by encouraging students to explore an important concept through the lens of their own life experiences. It also helps students develop a broader perspective by giving them the opportunity to explore how the same concept can affect others. What's more, the tool helps students build deep understanding through an active process of sharing and synthesizing ideas with their peers, rather than being told about the concept by the teacher.

What are the basic steps?

1. Organize students into groups of three. Number the students in each group (1, 2, 3).

2. Identify an important concept, theme, or issue within a topic or text you plan to teach. For the Gold Rush, you might pick *opportunity*. For Shakespeare's *Othello*, you might pick *jealousy*.

3. Use the three-round structure described below to have each group examine the concept, theme, or issue from three different perspectives—specifically, from the perspective of a PARTICIPANT (e.g., when they experienced or exhibited it), an OBSERVER, and a SUPPORTER.

Round 1: Ask students to think of a time when they were a PARTICIPANT (e.g., when they experienced or exhibited jealousy). Have them compare their thoughts and experiences with those of others in their group and look for commonalities. Student #1 should record key points, move to another group to share and compare ideas, and stay in that group for Round 2.

Round 2: Ask students to think of a time when they were an OBSERVER (e.g., when they observed someone being jealous). Have them share and discuss their experiences as they did in Round 1, except this time, have Student #2 take notes, switch groups, and share.

Round 3: Ask students to think of a time when they were a SUPPORTER (e.g., when they supported someone who was experiencing jealousy). Have them share and discuss their experiences as they did before, but have Student #3 take notes, switch groups, and share.

4. Instruct students to work with their final groups to synthesize what they learned and identify common attributes/understandings. ("Here is what we discovered about jealousy ...")

5. Ask students to apply what they learned to the original topic or text (e.g., "Compare your understanding of jealousy and its impact with its portrayal and outcome in *Othello*").

Note: Application tasks can take many forms; see the examples on pp. 29–30 for ideas.

How is this tool used in the classroom?

✔ To increase curiosity by encouraging students to connect personally with content

✔ To invite students to explore concepts using multiple perspectives

✔ To help students construct knowledge through conversations with their peers

EXAMPLE 1: Elementary social studies

As part of their social studies curriculum, fifth graders are learning about young people who changed the world. Before having students learn about the unbelievable courage of Malala Yousafzai, the youngest-ever Nobel Peace Prize laureate, the teacher wants students to explore their own experiences with courage using Think of a Time. The prompts for each round are shown below, along with the common ideas one student group generated for each round and after all three rounds were completed.

ROUND 1 (Participant): Think of a time when you were courageous. What was the situation? What did you do? How did you feel?

After sharing, one student group generated these common ideas based on their experiences:

- Being courageous can be hard.
- Being courageous makes you feel proud of yourself.
- Being courageous can be scary, but you can overcome your fears.

ROUND 2 (Observer): Think of a time when you observed someone else show courage. What did you see? What did you hear?

After sharing, one student group generated these common ideas based on their experiences:

- People are usually nervous before they need to show courage.
- People usually prepare themselves to show courage.
- Being courageous inspires other people to be courageous.

ROUND 3 (Supporter): Think of a time when you helped someone be courageous. What did you do? How did you help?

After sharing, one student group generated these common ideas based on their experiences:

- To help someone be courageous, you need to be a good listener.
- You can help by asking the person to focus on the good things that can happen as a result.

AFTER ALL THREE ROUNDS:

Here is a student group's final, synthesized ideas about courage:

- Courage doesn't mean you're not scared. It means you do something even when you are.
- We can help and inspire each other to be more courageous.
- Courage can help you accomplish your goals.

After reading about Malala, students use what they have learned about courage to engage in a whole-class discussion driven by these questions: Can one person's courage change the world? How is Malala's courage like our own courage and like the courage of people we know? How is her courage unique and extraordinary?

EXAMPLE 2: Primary

A primary-grade teacher is conducting a lesson on curiosity and how it can enhance learning. She begins by asking students to think of a time when they were curious and to share their experiences with the class. Rather than having students use the observer and supporter perspectives to explore further, the teacher poses three questions: "What kinds of things make us curious? What do we do when we're curious? How does it feel when we're curious?" After each question, the teacher gives students time to think and to share their ideas, which she records on the board. To synthesize the lesson, the teacher asks students, "How can curiosity help us learn?"

EXAMPLE 3: Secondary ELA

An English teacher used Think of a Time to help her students explore the concept of prejudice from the three perspectives prior to reading a set of poems by Harlem Renaissance poets. At the end of the lesson, students were asked to compare their perceptions of prejudice with that of the poems' narrators and discuss any new insights they gained as a result.

EXAMPLE 4: Secondary mathematics

A middle school math teacher knows that students' first serious encounters with algebra can be daunting, so she uses Think of a Time to help her algebra students understand the concept of a positive mindset and how it can help them succeed. She asks students to think of a time when they conquered a difficult learning challenge, when they observed someone else who overcame a difficult learning challenge, and when they helped someone overcome a difficult learning challenge. Afterward, the teacher and students work together to develop a set of guidelines for overcoming learning challenges. The guidelines become the very first page of students' notebooks, and the teacher encourages students to refer to them all year long to help them keep a positive mindset and overcome their challenges with algebra.

🌓 Teacher Talk

→ Note that individuals who have never experienced the issue from one or more of the perspectives can be asked to imagine what it might feel like instead.

→ Encourage everyone in the group to participate. Clarify that the conversations (and the notes from each round) should reflect the combined thoughts/experiences of the group as a whole.

→ Feel free to replace the three basic perspectives (participant/observer/supporter) with ones that better suit the purpose or content of your lesson. For example, you might ask students to explore westward expansion from three perspectives: settlers, Native Americans, and entrepreneurs.

→ To modify the tool for use with younger students, consider doing away with the three-round structure and discussing the three perspectives as a class instead.

→ When choosing a concept in Step 2, remember that it (as well as the experience of exploring it from three perspectives) should be chosen to help students develop a deeper understanding of the upcoming topic/text, to help students develop new perspectives/insights on the relevant material, and/or to make the topic/text more relatable or interesting (e.g., the Gold Rush is a foreign concept, but the concept of *opportunity* is one that all students can relate to).

What Comes to Mind?

What is it?

A quick and easy way to unlock students' background knowledge and use that knowledge to increase curiosity in the learning to come

What are the benefits of using this tool?

Unlocking students' prior knowledge about a topic before instruction begins can help increase curiosity about upcoming learning. Why? Because prior knowledge serves as the raw material students need to start thinking actively and curiously about the content to come. What do they already know about the topic they're going to be learning about? What questions or "wonderings" do they have about it? Does it evoke any particular feelings or associations? This tool encourages students to explore—and to fully "turn on"—their minds before learning. It also provides teachers with valuable pre-assessment information that they can use to teach more effectively. Best of all, the tool takes only a few minutes to implement in the classroom.

What are the basic steps?

1. Introduce the topic you are about to teach. ("For the next few days, we'll be learning about _____.")

2. Encourage students to explore their minds fully by asking themselves what they know, feel, and wonder about the topic. Have them record their responses on the reproducible organizer (p. 33) and/or share their responses aloud.

3. Review students' responses. Use what you learn about students' level of understanding to correct any factual errors or misconceptions and to adjust the entry point for instruction, if needed.

4. Use the additional information you gather to increase and sustain curiosity during instruction. Among other things, you might
   - Make connections between things students already know and content you're about to teach.
   - Incorporate students' questions into classroom discussions and lesson plans.
   - Encourage students to check and correct their facts and seek answers to their questions.
   - Discuss students' feelings about the topic.

🌑 Teacher Talk

➔ You can also use this tool to get students curious about how their minds work by asking this tongue-twisting question: "What do you know that you don't know you know?" Encourage them to think about why learners often believe they don't know much about a topic, only to find that when they stop and think, there is a lot more in their minds than they first thought. Discuss how this tool addresses this phenomenon.

How is this tool used in the classroom?

✔ To learn what students know, feel, and wonder about a topic before you begin teaching

✔ To help students unlock their curiosity before learning

✔ To adjust and improve instruction based on students' interests and needs

EXAMPLE: Elementary mathematics

Third graders are about to begin a unit on fractions. Their teacher uses What Comes to Mind? to help him pre-assess students' understanding and to help students approach the content with more active and curious minds. One student's completed organizer appears below.

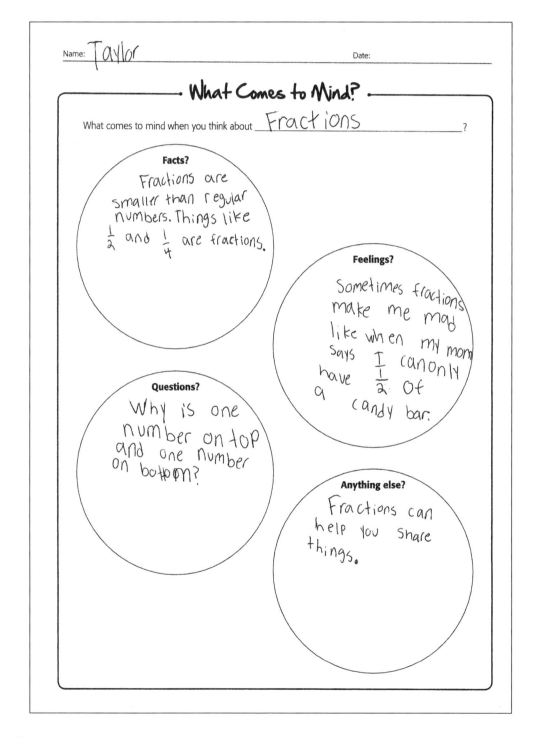

Name: _____ Date: _____

What Comes to Mind?

What comes to mind when you think about _____?

Facts?

Feelings?

Questions?

Anything else?

Fanning the Flame of Curiosity

Curiosity is seeing your way out of your place. It is looking beyond.

—Barbara M. Benedict, *Curiosity: A Cultural History of Early Modern Inquiry*

Promoting curiosity in children, especially those from environments of economic disadvantage, may be an important, underrecognized way to address the achievement gap.

—Prachi Shah, MD, pediatrician and researcher at the University of Michigan

Experiencing initial curiosity about a subject is a good start for learning—a great start, really—but what then? As it turns out, research on curiosity identifies another, deeper form of curiosity (sometimes called *informational* or *specific* curiosity) that drives us to keep exploring, keep turning over rocks, keep gathering information (Engel, 2015; Loewenstein, 1994). It's this form of curiosity that we associate with scientists, explorers, and experts.

We also know from the science of learning that such inquiry is what builds deep understanding. The drive to keep exploring—to seek out new ways of looking at challenges and new points of interest to pursue—keeps us focused on learning and draws us deeper into that learning. Stated simply, we only learn what we think about.

Perhaps we can do at least some of this without curiosity. After all, haven't we all had to grin and bear it as learners? Haven't we all clenched our teeth and relied on grit and perseverance to help us learn something? Yet, Angela Duckworth (2016), the researcher who brought the importance of grit to our attention, reminds us that grit consists of two elements: persistence and *passion*. And persistence without passion is just drudgery. In other words, it's far easier to learn something well when we're deeply engaged in learning it.

This chapter is designed to help you promote deep engagement so that the initial spark of curiosity turns into a flame of ongoing exploration and inquiry. With the tools in this chapter, you can ensure that your students "stay with it" to build deeper understanding. Even more, you can help students see that the goal of learning is not simply to memorize and recite facts, but rather to think critically as they get to the bottom of mysteries; make and test predictions; marshal evidence to support their ideas and positions; and construct knowledge through questioning, note making, and discussion. More generally, you'll be teaching your students how to think like detectives, scientists, researchers, historians, and explorers—people with insatiable curiosity about the world around them.

These are the six tools that will help you turn the initial spark of curiosity into a sustained flame of active learning:

1. **Before, During, After (BDA)** helps ensure that classroom questioning and discussion stimulate curiosity, promote the investigation of ideas, and lead to deep understanding.

2. **Inductive Learning** challenges students to construct meaning for themselves by analyzing information, making predictions, and then testing those predictions against new learning.

3. **K-W-L Jump-Start** is an enhanced version of the well-known K-W-L technique that encourages students to identify what they're curious about in relation to classroom topics—and seek out new learning that can help satisfy that curiosity.

4. **Mystery** captures and sustains curiosity by presenting students with a content-related mystery and challenging them to piece together clues to solve the mystery.

5. **Questions Are QUESTS** helps teachers turn classroom questioning into an ongoing "quest" for learning; it also teaches students a process for developing thoughtful responses to higher-order questions.

6. **Window Notes** empowers students to create notes driven by their own curiosity so that students engage deeply with what they're learning—rather than mindlessly copying information.

Before, During, After (BDA)

What is it?

A tool that ensures that classroom questioning achieves its full potential to stimulate curiosity, promote critical thinking, and build deep understanding

What are the benefits of using this tool?

Have you ever posed a question that you were sure was going to energize learning, only to see the energy dissipate almost immediately? One reason for this disappointing result is that it's not only the question that matters; it's also how you capture and sustain student curiosity throughout the questioning process. This tool helps teachers apply key research-based "curiosity principles" (Goodwin, 2018) to the questioning process. More specifically, it shows teachers how to set up and pose thoughtful questions to pique curiosity (BEFORE), use wait time and processing techniques to ensure active thinking (DURING), and use probing questions and prompts to help students expand on and refine their initial responses (AFTER).

What are the basic steps?

1. Develop a question that you want students to think about deeply.

   Note: It is important to have a clear purpose for your question: Why are you asking it? What do you hope students will learn/discover by exploring it? How will you assess student responses?

2. Prepare students for deep thinking BEFORE posing the question by providing context and piquing student curiosity. See Teacher Talk for tips on how to provide context and increase curiosity.

3. Pose the question to the class. Make sure all students understand the question, and provide wait time DURING the process to encourage students to think about possible responses.

4. Make students' covert thinking overt by having students generate their initial thoughts on paper.

   Tip: Have all students set aside a dedicated thinking journal or learning log at the beginning of the year as a place to collect and record their thoughts.

5. Allow students to share and compare their initial thoughts with a partner. Encourage students to listen to each other's responses carefully, look for similarities and differences in their thinking, and generate additional thoughts or select the best idea.

6. Invite students to share their ideas as a class. Call on a wide variety of students to ensure high levels of participation.

7. Use probing questions, paraphrasing, and participation prompts to help students evaluate and expand on their thinking AFTER they share their initial responses.
   - *Probe:* What is your evidence? How do you know that's so? And you think that because?
   - *Paraphrase:* Do I hear you saying ...? Do you mean ...?
   - *Participation prompts:* How many people agree? Who has a different point of view?

How is this tool used in the classroom?

✔ To train students to think deeply before, while, and after responding to questions

✔ To make the questioning process active

✔ To deepen responses through probing and participation techniques

EXAMPLE: Secondary history

Middle school students have been learning about the lead-up to the Civil War. Their teacher wants students to reflect on how the United States got to this point in its history and to weigh in on the question of whether the Civil War was inevitable. She uses the BDA process to conduct the lesson.

BEFORE: The teacher begins by asking students what the word *inevitable* means. What kinds of things do people talk about as being inevitable? She also asks students to draw on their own experiences. Have they ever experienced something inevitable? How did they know it was inevitable? When did they know it was inevitable? After drawing on students' experiences, she poses the question that will guide the lesson: "Was the Civil War inevitable?"

DURING: The teacher gives students time to review their notes and textbooks and to jot down their initial ideas. Students compare their ideas with a partner. In pairs, students must collect specific evidence that helps them support or refute the premise that the Civil War was inevitable.

AFTER: The teacher initiates a whole-class discussion in which students share and justify their ideas. She uses a wide variety of prompts, directed questions, and participation techniques to help students analyze their initial ideas and deepen their understanding.

Student 1: I believe that the Civil War was inevitable.

Teacher: What evidence leads you to believe that?

Student 1: I guess I should have said that the Civil War was inevitable once Lincoln was elected. When you look at how quickly the southern states seceded before Lincoln was even inaugurated, that makes it pretty clear what was going to happen.

Teacher: Do others agree or disagree?

Student 2: I agree. And once the South seceded, there was nothing Lincoln could do to bring them back except to use force. So it was inevitable after that.

Teacher: What about before Lincoln was elected? Was it inevitable before that happened?

Student 3: I think it was, yes.

Teacher: And what's your evidence?

Student 3: The Kansas-Nebraska Act. Once Kansas and Nebraska were allowed to decide for themselves if they wanted to be slave states, the Civil War became inevitable.

Teacher: And you think this because?

Student 3: Because the North felt like the South was breaking an important promise, and this was just too much for many Northerners to take.

Student 4: I think it goes even further back because the North and the South were really two different countries all along. They had different views on slavery, different economies, different . . .

 **Teacher Talk**

➜ To better prepare students for the question, provide background information or a context that will make the question more meaningful and interesting when you pose it.

Sample language: Have you ever heard of a mixed blessing? It means that something is both positive and negative at the same time. Take cars, for example. They get us where we want to go whenever we want. But they also create huge amounts of pollution, and car accidents cause thousands of deaths every year. Today, we'll be exploring a different mixed blessing: fracking.

➜ To increase student interest in your question, consider how you can use the "Eight Cs of Engagement" (Silver & Perini, 2010) to make your question especially intriguing. Some of the Cs, along with questions that engage these Cs, include

- **C**HOICE: Is *Huckleberry Finn* best described as a study in equality, morality, or individualism?

- **C**ONTROVERSY: Agree or disagree: There should be a minimum age requirement to carry a cell phone.

- **C**REATIVITY: What if Thomas Edison had never lived? How would your life be different?

- Personal **C**ONNECTIONS: Have you ever been a victim of prejudice? How did it affect you?

➜ Posing a question is different than asking a question. Posing is an invitation to explore possible ideas and responses. To help emphasize this point in the classroom, explain to students that the root of the word *question* is *quest*. A quest is a journey, a search for truth. Instead of questioning, invite the class to go "questing." (See Questions Are QUESTS, pp. 55–57.)

➜ Pausing several seconds after asking a question to give students time to think before responding and to refine their thinking is called "wait time." When students have more time to think about their responses before they actually respond, they tend to participate more in class, think more deeply, and generate more thoughtful responses (Rowe, 1972; Tobin, 1987). Of course, it's not just the wait time that counts; it's also what students do with the time. By inviting students to write down their initial thoughts, you help them get their ideas out in the open; by allowing them to share their ideas with another student, you help them test and refine their ideas—and gain new perspectives.

➜ The probing and participation prompts/questions below enhance student discussions. Notice that they encourage thinking rather than looking for correct answers.

- Share your thinking.

- What are your ideas?

- Can you give me an example?

- That's an interesting way to think. How did you arrive at that idea?

- What's behind your idea? Can you explain your reasoning?

- Does anyone have a different idea?

- How many agree? How many disagree? Who's unsure?

Inductive Learning

What is it?

A tool that empowers students to actively construct meaning for themselves by analyzing information, classifying it into groups, using it to make informed predictions, and testing those predictions against new learning

What are the benefits of using this tool?

Education pioneer Hilda Taba helped inspire a generation of educators to make the shift from learning as passive acquisition "to learning as a way of inquiring and thinking" (Taba, Durkin, Fraenkel, & McNaughton, 1971, p. 1). Taba's ideas are as relevant today as ever—especially for educators seeking tried-and-true ways to ensure that curiosity flourishes in the classroom. Inductive Learning is based on Taba's influential work. It promotes active learning by challenging students to make meaning of the content for themselves through induction, or the process of developing a general, big-picture understanding by searching for patterns in the specifics. It also asks students to make predictions about content, which helps sustain curiosity because "the brain's permanent wiring dictates the need to find out if a prediction is correct" (McTighe & Willis, 2019, p. 58).

What are the basic steps?

1. Identify the big ideas/themes in a topic or text you're about to teach. Generate fifteen to forty terms, phrases, or other items (e.g., images, quotations, objects) that relate to, or are examples of, those big ideas. Be sure to generate multiple items for each big idea.

2. Break students into teams. Distribute the items you generated to each team, and help students comprehend what they've been given. ("What does this word mean? What is this a picture of?")

3. Ask students to organize the items into groups using whatever criteria they want. (Clarify that the same item can go in multiple groups.) Emphasize that there's no "right" way to group the items or right number of groups to form, and encourage students to explore different options.

4. Have students record their groups on the provided organizer (p. 45) or on plain paper if they need more room. Then have them give each group a descriptive label that explains what the grouped items have in common. (Students should be ready to explain their groups and labels if asked.)

5. Pose questions that will help students improve and expand their initial groups/labels. Encourage students to look for relationships they hadn't previously noticed, devise more descriptive labels for their groups, and/or combine their original groups into larger, more inclusive ones.

6. Have students use their groups and labels to generate (then share) predictions or conclusions.

7. Help students revise their predictions/conclusions as needed in light of new learning.

How is this tool used in the classroom?

✔ To promote inquiry and inductive thinking in the classroom

✔ To encourage students to make and test predictions

✔ To help students discover big ideas and concepts

Inductive Learning can be used for different purposes and at different points in an instructional sequence. Examples 1–4 show how the tool can be used to engage students in generating and testing predictions about important topics or texts. In Example 5, you'll see how the grouping and labeling process can help students arrive at thoughtful conclusions. And in Teacher Talk, you'll learn how Inductive Learning can be used as a review tool at the end of an instructional unit.

EXAMPLE 1: Elementary ELA

An elementary reading teacher uses Inductive Learning on a regular basis because it engages students in making pre-reading predictions that raise their curiosity ("I wonder if my predictions will pan out …") and promote active reading ("What information in the text supports or refutes my predictions?"). Today, he's using the tool to spark interest and introduce key themes before having students read a modern retelling of the famous American tall tale *Pecos Bill*.

In preparation for the lesson, he identified themes that he believed were central to the story and that would capture students' interest—themes like romance, danger, heroes, and the Wild West. He then selected words from the text that he believed would illustrate and help students discover these themes before they began reading. These are the words that he selected:

Texas	moon	Arizona
Pecos Bill	fight	ceremony
bronco	stars	cyclone
tough	headlock	pasture
Slue-foot Sue	coyote	The Hell's Gate Gang
cowboy	scorpion	tarantula
New Mexico	ranch	lightning
campfire	punch	mountain lion
strong	save	rescue
married	sweetheart	defend
drought	lovestruck	Death Valley

On the day of the lesson, the teacher challenged students to organize these words into groups, give each group a descriptive label, and use their labeled groups to generate predictions about the story.

The organizer below shows how a team of students grouped and labeled the words (and successfully identified some of the story's major themes). The organizer also shows how these students improved their initial groups/labels in response to their teacher's probing questions.

- In response to the question "What *kinds* of weather terms are in your weather group?," for example, students changed the name of that group from *weather* to DANGEROUS *weather*.
- When asked if any groups could be combined into a larger, more inclusive one, students merged their *dangerous weather*, *scary animals*, and *fighting* groups into a "dangerous things" group.

These students used their groups and labels to make predictions about the story, its setting, and its characters. Here are some of the predictions they generated:

> We predict that . . .
> 1. Pecos Bill and Slue-foot Sue will fall in love and get married.
> 2. This will be a story about cowboys and heroes out West.
> 3. Pecos Bill is a strong and tough cowboy who will rescue and save someone.
> 4. Pecos Bill will encounter many dangers, like cyclones, scorpions, gangs, and fights.

After sharing and discussing their predictions as a class, students began reading. Because they were curious to see whether their predictions panned out, they dove into the story eagerly, seeking out details that supported or refuted their ideas. When they finished, the teacher engaged them in a discussion about which of their predictions were most accurate and why.

EXAMPLE 2: Secondary science

A physics teacher uses Inductive Learning on the first day of school to get students engaged and interested in the learning to come. She distributes index cards containing terms (e.g., velocity, acceleration, friction), images (e.g., roller coaster, curve ball in motion, drag race), and word problems that reflect core concepts from the course. After explaining/defining unfamiliar terms and images, she challenges students to use the cards to try and figure out what they'll be learning about over the course of the year. Students work in teams to group the cards, label their groups, and use their labeled groups to make some predictions. After sharing their ideas as a class, students are challenged to search the course syllabus for evidence that supports or refutes their predictions.

EXAMPLE 3: Secondary history

A middle school history teacher uses Inductive Learning to introduce—and engage students in making predictions about—an ancient civilization they're about to study. He thinks about the big ideas he wants students to understand and remember about this civilization, and he collects terms and images of artifacts that reflect and relate to those big ideas. After grouping the terms/artifacts and labeling their groups, students use their labeled groups to make predictions about the civilization's values and beliefs, accomplishments, economy, way of life, and more. For example:

• A group containing religious artifacts, images of temples, and the names of gods and goddesses (students labeled it "religion") leads students to predict that the civilization they're about to study was a polytheistic one that valued religion highly.

• An "architecture" group containing images of large and complex structures (temples, pyramids, tombs) leads students to predict that the civilization had an advanced understanding of architectural and construction/engineering principles.

EXAMPLE 4: Secondary art

A middle school art teacher uses Inductive Learning at the start of an art history unit to preview and get his students curious about the different artists and artistic styles they'll be learning about. He divides students into teams and gives each team a set of "art postcards" containing paintings from different time periods and artists. Students are instructed to examine the paintings carefully, look for common attributes (subject matter, style, technique, etc.), and group the paintings accordingly. They're then challenged to use their labeled groups to predict which paintings might've been painted at the same time period or by the same artist. To keep students actively engaged, the teacher has them check and correct their predictions as they learn more about the characteristics and styles of different artists and art movements over the course of the unit.

EXAMPLE 5: Elementary science

A third-grade teacher uses Inductive Learning to help his students see how organisms can be organized into groups based on common characteristics or features—an authentic task that real-world scientists engage in. Instead of giving students a list of organisms to group and label, the teacher "keeps things authentic" by inviting them to generate their own list during a field trip to a local Florida nature preserve. At the preserve, students continue to engage in "real science" by carefully observing, sketching, and making notes about the organisms they see, both in the field and on informational placards. Back in the classroom, students use their notes to organize the organisms they observed into related groups, some of which are shown on the next page.

Sharing their groups and labels as a class helps students conclude that organisms can be classified in many different ways—for example, by physical features (e.g., animals that are green, animals with wings, animals with two legs), by where they live (e.g., water, air, soil), by how they behave (e.g., how they move or eat), or by using "familiar categories" (e.g., plants, reptiles, mammals, insects).

🌓 Teacher Talk

→ To scaffold the group-and-label process for young learners or first-time users of this tool, you might have students conduct a closed sort. (In a closed sort, you provide the categories and students sort the items into these predefined categories rather than creating their own classification system.) When students are ready to use the tool as written, have them practice grouping and labeling familiar items (e.g., items at a grocery store) before introducing more challenging ones.

→ Teachers typically generate the items that students will group and label, so that students stay focused on important themes and ideas. But they don't have to. Students can generate (or help you generate) items instead, as shown in Example 5. Feel free to supplement students' ideas as needed.

→ When developing an Inductive Learning lesson around a piece of literature (as in Example 1), it's important to present the words in random order, rather than in the order they appear in the text. Include words that reflect a variety of story elements (characters, character traits, setting, plot), so that students will be able to make predictions about each of these critical elements. To see how this looks, examine the teacher's words (p. 41) and the students' predictions (p. 42) from Example 1.

→ Inviting student to generate and test predictions is a great strategy for sparking and sustaining interest. But it's not just the "testing your predictions" component of this tool that gets students curious; the initial list of items sparks curiosity in and of itself. How? When students see the list, they immediately start wondering how the items are related and what they might reveal about the topic.

→ Inductive Learning is a great lesson/unit opener, because the predictions that students generate serve to drive and motivate new learning. But it also works well as an end-of-unit review technique. To use the tool for review, challenge students to group and label key terms from the unit. The goal is for them to show that they understand the content deeply by creating a kind of conceptual map of the unit. The labels represent the big ideas/concepts; the terms inside are the supporting details.

→ The items that you give students to group should be specific rather than general or conceptual, so that students can induce the bigger ideas/concepts by grouping and labeling those items. If you want students to construct an agriculture group, for example, you should give them items that are related to/examples of *agriculture* (e.g., crops, tractor) rather than the word *agriculture* itself.

Name: _____   Date: _____

Group & Label Organizer

K-W-L Jump-Start

What is it?

A variation of Ogle's (1986) popular K-W-L technique that uses concrete prompts to help students jump-start and focus their thinking about what they **K**now and **W**ant to know about a given topic—and a redesigned visual organizer to help students connect their initial ideas/questions to what they **L**earn

What are the benefits of using this tool?

The K-W-L process has great potential, since inviting students to reflect on what they know, want to know, and learn about a topic has the power to boost curiosity, motivation, and achievement. When teachers use K-W-L in the classroom, however, it often "stalls out" because students write very little about what they know and want to know—or because students generate knowledge and questions that aren't relevant to the upcoming learning. This enhanced version of K-W-L addresses these problems and helps K-W-L fulfill its potential by using concrete prompts (words, pictures, questions) to jump-start and focus student thinking. The tool also helps teachers sustain student interest and energy by reminding them to address—and encourage students to seek answers to—the questions that students generate.

What are the basic steps?

1. Identify the topic of an upcoming lesson or unit. Fill the "jump-start your thinking" box of a K-W-L Jump-Start organizer (p. 49) with words and/or images that you think will help students retrieve relevant prior knowledge and generate on-target Want-to-know questions in Step 5.

2. Present the topic and organizer to students. Instruct students to record anything they **K**now or *think* they know about the topic on their organizers.

3. Encourage students to use the jump-start box to spark and focus their thinking. Pose direct questions to further jump-start students' memories. For a lesson on pandas, for example, you might ask, "Do you know anything about where pandas live? What they eat? What color they are?"

4. Have students share their ideas as a class. Encourage them to add shared ideas to their organizers.

5. Ask students what they **W**ant to know about the topic at hand. Generate a list as a class. Then invite students to record items from the list that interest them personally on their individual organizers.

6. Adapt your instructional plans to accommodate students' existing knowledge and interests. Challenge students to seek out answers to their questions independently as well. Provide—or help students identify—resources that might help them. ("Where or how could you find that out?")

7. Have students revisit their organizers regularly to record what they **L**earn, and check/correct the accuracy of their original ideas. Encourage them to reflect on the ways their knowledge has grown.

How is this tool used in the classroom?

✔ To preview content, activate/assess prior knowledge, and spark interest at the start of a lesson

✔ To encourage students to generate (and seek out responses to) questions that interest them

✔ To boost curiosity and motivation by designing instruction with students' interests in mind

EXAMPLE 1: Secondary history

Below is the K-W-L Jump-Start organizer that a middle school student completed during an Age of Exploration unit. Notice how the word bank that the teacher provided served to focus the background knowledge that the student retrieved and help the student generate relevant questions (word bank terms are underlined). Notice also how the student used check marks to indicate the accuracy of his initial ideas and arrows to connect his initial ideas and questions to his new learning.

Use these words to jump-start your thinking about the Age of Exploration:

New World	Portugal	Christopher Columbus	Spain	Vasco da Gama	Far East
colonial empires	discovery	Native Americans	explorers	Bartolomeu Dias	navigation
conquistadors	trade routes	Cape of Good Hope	disease	gold, silver, spices	maps

---

What do I think I Know?

- People believed the Earth was flat before Columbus sailed to the New World.
- ✓ Explorers were looking for new trade routes.
- ✓ Explorers wanted to find gold, silver, and spices so that they could get rich.

What do I Want to know?

- How did the explorers know where they were going in the middle of the ocean?
- If Native Americans were already here, why do people say Columbus discovered America?

What have I Learned?

- It turns out that most people, at least the educated ones, knew the Earth was round. But they still didn't think Columbus could get to the Far East by sailing west.
- Instead of reaching the Far East, Columbus hit the New World. That's why people say he discovered it.
- The land route to the Far East was controlled by the Ottoman Empire, so Europeans began looking for new sea routes to get there. The rounding of the Cape of Good Hope by Bartolomeu Dias was a major milestone.
- Some spices were worth more than gold! They used spices for medicine and to flavor their food.
- Explorers used the stars and sun to guide them. They also used maps and technology like mariner's astrolabes to help them figure out where they were.

EXAMPLE 2: Preschool

A pre-K teacher used this tool at the start of a "preparing for kindergarten" lesson so that she could see what her students already knew and what questions they had. She used questions rather than words or images to help students retrieve prior knowledge and generate on-target questions—and she had students complete the K-W-L process as a class, rather than using individual organizers. Some of the questions that she posed are shown on the next page, along with responses that students generated during the *K* and *W* phases. Students' responses and questions were then used to focus the lesson.

Questions the teacher posed to jump-start student thinking:

- What kinds of activities do you think you'll do? What do you think you'll learn?
- What do you think a kindergarten classroom looks like?
- How do you think you'll get to kindergarten every day?
- How old do you think kids in kindergarten are?
- Do you have any questions about the bus? The activities? What you'll do each day?

What we THINK WE KNOW about kindergarten	What we WANT TO KNOW about kindergarten
I get to meet a new teacher.	Are we going to do fun activities?
I will meet new friends.	Will we have snack time?
You get to play outside.	What will we do there?
I think I will get to do science and explore.	Will we get to go on the playground every day?
I think I will learn ABCs and counting.	Does kindergarten have blocks and Magna-Tiles?
I think kindergarten is a big room with toys.	Why do I have to go to a new school?
You have to go to a different school.	Will the big kids tease me?
I will get to go on a school bus.	Do I have to go on a school bus?
You have to be five years old to go there.	Will the school bus have seat belts?
There is a cafeteria to get your food.	Will the bus driver be nice to me?

🌐 Teacher Talk

→ Personal experience has taught us that asking students to record not just what they know, but what they *think they know*—and emphasizing that it's ok to be unsure—increases participation. Asking students to record what they think rather than what they know (Step 2) has also been found to increase the number of ideas that they generate (Crowther & Cannon, 2004).

→ We redesigned the traditional three-column K-W-L organizer so that the *K* and *W* boxes are on the left and the *L* box is on the right. As shown in Example 1, this redesign lets students connect what they *Learn* with both their prior knowledge (from the *K* box) and their questions (from the *W* box).

→ When using this tool with younger students, we suggest completing the organizer as a class and posing lots of questions to help students retrieve relevant background knowledge. See Example 2.

→ Filling in the "jump-start your thinking" box with topic-specific words is a great way to introduce students to the critical vocabulary terms for an upcoming lesson or unit.

→ Help students recognize that they know more than they think about a topic by posing silly or exaggerated questions that they *will* be able to answer. If students say they know nothing about crocodiles, for example, you might ask questions like, "Is a crocodile bigger than a mouse? As big as a skyscraper? Is a crocodile a plant? Is a crocodile purple?" Besides generating laughs, questions like these will help students retrieve useful factual knowledge that they can then record in the "know" column. (Crocodiles are big, but not as big as skyscrapers. They're animals, not plants …)

Name: _____

Date: _____

Topic: _____

K-W-L Jump-Start

Words or pictures to jump-start your thinking:

What I think I **K**now	What I **L**earned
What I **W**ant to know	

Save this handout, and add to it over time. Record what you learn, add more questions, and check your original ideas. If you find that any of your original ideas about the topic were incorrect or incomplete, go ahead and fix them! If any of your original ideas were correct, mark them with a ✓.

Mystery

What is it?

A tool that hooks and holds students' curiosity by engaging them in solving content-related mysteries; students use teacher-provided clues to develop and test possible solutions

What are the benefits of using this tool?

Few things awaken curiosity better than a good mystery. By presenting students with unusual phenomena and other content-related "head-scratchers" that beg for explanations, this tool capitalizes on the power of mysteries to rouse the mind to life. But the tool does more than capture interest; it engages students in generating and testing hypotheses. This process of developing, testing, and refining hypotheses keeps curiosity levels high, develops deep understanding, and builds a host of critical thinking skills, including analyzing data, synthesizing information, and supporting ideas with evidence. It also leads to higher levels of achievement (Dean, Hubbell, Pitler, & Stone, 2012).

What are the basic steps?

1. Identify an event, phenomenon, or concept that you want students to understand and explain. Frame it as a mystery that students will need to investigate/solve (e.g., "How is it possible that a giant metal boat can stay afloat when this tiny piece of metal sinks in a glass of water?").

2. Develop a clear idea of the solution/explanation you want your students to generate. List the big ideas students will need to understand in order to arrive at the solution you have in mind.

3. Create a set of clues that will enable students to discover the solution and the big ideas that underpin that solution. Clues can take any form you want—data tables, images, maps, sound clips, factual information in sentence form, etc. See Teacher Talk for more on generating clues.

4. Divide students into teams. Present the mystery, give each team a set of clues, and tell students to
   - Examine the clues carefully. Group related clues together, and give each group a descriptive label. (Clarify that students may place the same clue in more than one group.)
   - Summarize the key ideas from each group. (Think: What are the clues telling you?)
   - Identify connections between or among clue groups. (Do you see common threads or themes?)
   - Think about how the clues/groups are connected to the mystery as a whole.
   - Generate a tentative solution that's supported by the clues. Be ready to share and defend it.

5. Invite students to share their ideas and solutions—and the clue evidence that supports those ideas/solutions—both as they work and at the end of the lesson. Use probing questions to help students evaluate and refine their ideas. See Teacher Talk for specific suggestions.

6. Assess and reinforce students' grasp of the relevant content at the end of the lesson by asking students what they learned and by reviewing the critical concepts/ideas as a class.

How is this tool used in the classroom?

✔ To help students learn critical content in a way that captures and holds curiosity

✔ To provide an authentic and engaging context for students to generate and test hypotheses

✔ To develop students' ability to analyze and interpret data—and support ideas with evidence

Teachers across content areas use this tool to help students generate possible explanations of mysterious phenomena or observations. Mysteries are usually presented as *why* or *how* questions. Multiple sample questions are shown below, along with two fleshed-out classroom examples.

- Why is it better to sneeze into your elbow than into your hand?

- How did an untrained colonial militia defeat the mighty British army?

- In 2010, a fossil of a giant whale was discovered in a desert in Peru. How did it get there?

- How is it possible that airplanes don't fall out of the sky even though they're so heavy?

- Why is George Washington considered a great war hero when he lost more battles than he won?

- How is it possible that burning a forest can be good for its health?

- Why was there an explosion of mystery novels and detective stories in the Victorian era?

- What painters painted and how they painted it changed dramatically between the Middle Ages and the Renaissance. Why? What explains the change?

- There's only one correct order in which to perform mathematical operations. Can you discover what it is just by examining these clues?

EXAMPLE 1: Elementary social studies

A fifth-grade teacher uses the essential question, "Does the person make the times or do the times make the person?" throughout the year to help students explore the achievements of historical figures. Today, students are using this question to explore the legacy of Jackie Robinson. To raise student curiosity, the teacher begins by framing the lesson as a mystery: Many African American baseball players had been talented enough to play in the Major Leagues, but none did until Jackie Robinson joined the Brooklyn Dodgers in 1947. She tells students that their job is to figure out the answer to three questions: "Why Jackie Robinson? Why 1947? Why the Brooklyn Dodgers?"

The teacher organizes students into teams and challenges them to solve the mystery using clues that she provides (twenty slips of paper, each with a brief bit of relevant information drawn from biographical excerpts and articles). Students are instructed to organize related clues into groups and use the groups they create to develop some possible hypotheses for why the conditions were right for Jackie Robinson to break the color barrier in 1947. One such clue group is shown below, along with the hypothesis that students generated as a result of grouping the clues.

> Clue 2: The United States was involved in World War II from 1941 until 1945.

> Clue 6: During World War II, President Franklin Roosevelt issued an order that allowed all Americans to work in the defense industry. As a result, many African Americans got higher-paying jobs and worked alongside white co-workers for the first time.

> Clue 11: During World War II, many more African Americans served in combat roles than ever before.

We hypothesize that the time was right for Jackie Robinson in 1947 because World War II helped African Americans get new jobs and opportunities that they weren't allowed to have before.

Additional clue groups (not shown) lead students to hypothesize that it was not only the times that contributed to Jackie Robinson's rise to success, but also his athletic ability, his personality, and Branch Rickey's (the Dodgers' general manager) beliefs about equality.

After a round of discussion in which students share their hypotheses and the "clue evidence" that supports them, students read an article about Jackie Robinson and his breakthrough season. Students use the article to test and refine their hypotheses. ("How do the ideas you generated compare with those in the text?")

EXAMPLE 2: Secondary science

Instead of telling students why scientists think dinosaurs became extinct, a high school teacher challenges them to generate plausible explanations (hypotheses) on their own. To spark their interest, he frames the dinosaur disappearance as an intriguing mystery for them to solve: "We've just learned that the dinosaurs dominated the earth for over 150 million years. So how is it possible that they became extinct? Today, you'll get a chance to investigate and solve that mystery using a set of clues that I will give you."

The teacher divides students into teams of four and presents each team with an identical set of thirty-five clues. (To create the clues, he pulled bits of information from an article that presented a commonly accepted explanation for the dinosaurs' demise.) As students begin working to analyze and group the clues, the teacher walks around to listen in on, probe, and guide their thinking.

Students in one of the teams notice that there are multiple clues about tropical plants—and they group those clues accordingly. They create a plankton group as well, as shown below.

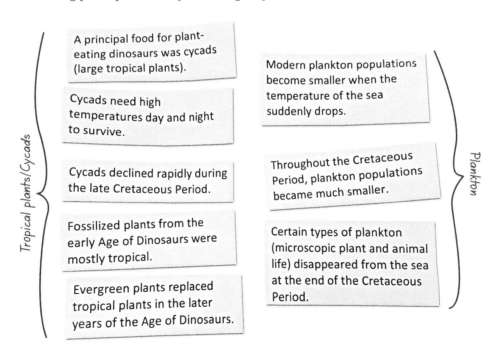

When they examine their groups more closely, the students notice some common themes. They notice, for example, that clues in both groups highlight changes in population that occurred during the Cretaceous Period. (Populations of tropical plants and plankton both declined rapidly.)

They also find multiple temperature-related clues—clues that lead them to hypothesize that a drop in temperature was what caused the cycad and plankton populations to decline.

When their teacher asks how the clues they've examined so far might relate to the mystery of why the dinosaurs died out, these students hypothesize that a shortage of food, triggered by a drop in temperature, might have caused the dinosaurs' demise. ("We learned that cycads declined, and cycads were a major source of food for the dinosaurs.")

But what might have caused such a drop in temperature? After grouping and labeling additional clues (not shown), team members hypothesize that the drop in temperature was caused by a giant meteor that hit the earth and created a large cloud of dust that blocked out sunlight.

At the end of class, after teams have shared and critiqued each other's hypotheses (and supporting clues), the teacher challenges students to develop a brief, written explanation—backed by clue evidence—that synthesizes the class's ideas about the factors that led to the demise of the dinosaurs. One student's explanation can be viewed at www.ThoughtfulClassroom.com/Tools.

Variation: Yes/No Inquiry

This variation on Mystery is adapted from the work of J. R. Suchman (1966). Like Mystery, Yes/No Inquiry involves presenting students with an intriguing phenomenon or mystery and challenging them to solve/explain it. The technique differs from Mystery in that students use yes/no questions that *they* develop (rather than teacher-provided clues) to gather data that can help them.

In its simplest form, Yes/No Inquiry can be used to challenge students to identify a "mystery item" that their teacher is thinking of (a concept, event, person, or place that students have recently learned about). Rather than simply guessing what the item is, students are encouraged—and taught how— to ask yes/no questions that focus on its critical attributes. An elementary teacher, for example, might challenge students to "figure out what shape I'm thinking of" by helping them develop yes/no questions about the shape's critical attributes (e.g., Does the shape have sides? Does it have more than three sides? Does it have parallel sides? Does it have angles of equal size?).

The same process of asking yes/no questions can also be used by students to generate and test hypotheses about "mysterious" phenomena that they observe. A science teacher, for example, might challenge students to use yes/no questions to generate a plausible explanation for something they observe during a demonstration (e.g., Why, when ice cubes are placed in two identical-looking beakers filled with clear liquid, do the ice cubes float in one of the beakers but sink in the other?). At the end of the demonstration, students would be instructed to

- Record everything they know about the situation.
- Generate one or more hypotheses to explain what they observed (e.g., "The liquids in the two beakers must be different").
- Develop yes/no questions that would help them test their hypotheses and pose those questions to the teacher (e.g., "If I moved the ice cubes that sank to the other beaker, would they float?")
- Develop what they believe is the best explanation for the phenomenon.

🌀 Teacher Talk

➔ Here are some things to keep in mind when generating your clues:

- Clues should contain information that will help students generate their own ideas and solutions; they shouldn't *tell* students the solution. Check that the clues you generate give students enough information to develop the generalizations and conclusions you expect them to make.

- Clues can be derived from primary or secondary sources—and they can be copied directly or rewritten/summarized for length or age-appropriateness. You might, for example, reprint an entry from a captain's log or summarize information from an article on the whaling industry.

- Build different types of clues into your lessons (e.g., maps, tables, or images in addition to written-out factual information) so that students get practice interpreting different forms of data.

➔ Use probing questions to help students articulate, evaluate, and expand their thinking, both as they work (Step 4) and when they're sharing their ideas as a class (Step 5). For example: How did you group the clues and why? What did you learn from each group? Do you see any connections between groups? How might the information from these groups relate to the mystery as a whole? What solution did you develop? What clue evidence supports this solution? Are there any clues you've failed to account for or that contradict your proposed solution? Is your logic sound?

➔ Help students evaluate the explanations that they and their classmates generate (Step 5) by having them review each team's ideas, identify potential issues (e.g., flaws in logic, failure to account for critical information, information that doesn't fit), and decide which explanation is best supported by the evidence. Alternatively, you can have students compare their solutions with the actual solution. ("Read this article. How does the author's explanation compare with yours?")

➔ Clarify that it's not a problem if students generate a different solution/response than you had in mind at the start of the activity as long as their response is supported by solid evidence. In fact, you can use students' differing solutions as a way to introduce the idea that there are many instances where multiple hypotheses are plausible and supported by evidence.

➔ At first, some teachers wonder if the time it takes to plan a Mystery lesson is worth it. In our experience, once teachers see the curiosity and engagement that the tool generates—and its ability to promote active, authentic learning—they don't tend to ask the "is it worth it" question anymore. To reduce the workload, collaborate with teachers at your school to develop and share Mystery lessons. And remember that once you've created a Mystery lesson, you can reuse it every year.

➔ Don't let the process of developing a good Mystery lesson scare you. Just remember the four "Es": Pick any Event or phenomenon that you want students to be able to explain; identify the Explanation or cause behind the event; gather the Evidence (facts, details, data, etc.) that students will need to construct the explanation; withhold the explanation, and Engage students in using the evidence to construct it on their own.

➔ Instead of *giving* students clues, you can have students discover the relevant information (clues) for themselves. To do this, set up "discovery stations" where students complete a task (e.g., watch a video, make observations, perform an experiment) and jot down what they learn.

Questions Are QUESTS

What is it?

A tool that helps teachers turn classroom questioning into learning "quests" and teaches students a thinking process for developing thoughtful responses to higher-order questions

What are the benefits of using this tool?

Many of the words associated with the act of questioning (*question*, *query*, *inquiry*) come from roots meaning "to seek" or "to go in search of." This makes perfect sense. After all, only the simplest questions have answers that are right at hand. Good questions require students to think deeply and to search actively—to quest—for information that will help them construct a quality response. Questions Are QUESTS helps teachers develop "quest-worthy" questions and establish a classroom culture that encourages students to pursue new learning related to those questions. It also helps students build the habits of sophisticated thinkers who understand that good responses are not ready-made, but are developed and refined over time through ongoing learning and discussion.

What are the basic steps?

1. Review a unit or lesson sequence you will be teaching. Identify the big ideas and the key learning targets you expect students to meet.

2. Develop a quest-worthy question for students to explore during the unit. A quest-worthy question will spark curiosity, promote inquiry into the big ideas of the unit, and require students to build and refine their responses over time. See the sample questions on p. 56 for ideas.

3. Present the question to students at the beginning of the unit.

   Note: You can make the question more curiosity-inducing and more meaningful for students by providing background knowledge and/or a context for the question. For example, see how the teacher in the classroom example on p. 56 sets up her question about predicting the weather.

4. Explain that students will be using the QUESTS process to go in search of learning and develop their responses over time. Use the handout on p. 57 to introduce and model the steps before having students use the process to tackle the question you presented in Step 3.

5. Prepare students to develop their responses by facilitating relevant learning activities, helping students collect important information, and giving students regular opportunities to share and refine their ideas with their classmates.

6. Ask students to construct a response that synthesizes what they have learned.

7. Encourage students to keep the handout in their notebooks and to use the QUESTS process to help them develop high-quality responses. Reinforce that the steps in QUESTS are the behaviors that good thinkers use to craft better, more sophisticated responses.

How is this tool used in the classroom?

✔ To develop quest-worthy questions

✔ To teach students a process for developing deeper, more thoughtful responses to questions

✔ To establish a classroom culture that promotes inquiry, discussion, and in-depth learning

The Questions Are QUESTS process is driven by a rich, quest-worthy question that will inspire students to go in search of new learning that can help them build their response. Examples of quest-worthy questions are shown below, followed by a fleshed-out classroom example showing how a teacher guides students through the QUESTS process.

• Why do plants grow in places where people haven't planted them?

• What's the difference between using statistics and abusing statistics?

• How is a colony like a child?

• How have writers from a wide variety of cultures contributed to our understanding of the American experience?

• How are functions used in the real world?

• Is cosmetology more of an art or a science?

EXAMPLE: Elementary science

A fourth-grade teacher begins a unit on weather by providing some background knowledge. She tells students that even though today's meteorologists have advanced equipment and technology to help them, they still get the weather forecast wrong sometimes. She then poses a question designed to provoke their curiosity and guide the QUESTS process: "Why is the weather so hard to predict?"

The teacher works with students to "question the question" to help them recognize that it is asking them to develop an explanation, or provide reasons why the weather is hard to predict. Then, over the course of the unit, the teacher leads students on a quest to build their understanding and develop and refine their responses. More specifically, she

• Encourages students to tap into their prior knowledge and offer their initial responses to the question. Initial student responses include "Because predicting the future is not really possible" and "Because storms form too fast."

• Engages students in a learning sequence that helps them develop their understanding of the weather and the factors involved in predicting it.

• Has the class track the weather for two weeks.

• Allows students to meet regularly in small groups to discuss their learning and refine their initial ideas and responses.

At the end of the unit, the teacher makes the process of responding to the question more authentic and engaging by asking students to imagine that they are a local weatherperson who gets lots of angry calls whenever the forecast is not perfectly accurate. Taking the position of the local weatherperson, students have to defend themselves by explaining to the public why it is difficult to predict the weather perfectly.

Questions Are QUESTS

Question the question.	Examine the question closely. What is it asking? What kind of thinking will it take to respond to it? Will you be developing an explanation, making a comparison, developing an argument, thinking speculatively, etc.?
Understand that you are on a "quest."	You will be going on a collaborative search with your classmates for ideas and information that can help you respond to the question. The idea is not to find a quick answer; the idea is to build and refine your response over time as you learn more during the unit.
Establish what you know.	Your prior knowledge is often a powerful tool to help you begin building your response. What do you already know about the topic of the question? Jot down anything you know or have learned that might help you respond to the question.
Search for information and ideas.	As you learn more during the unit, be on the lookout for any ideas or information that can help you develop and add to your response. Make notes and/or pictures to capture important information and to help you recall what you have learned when you need it.
Talk about your ideas.	We learn better when we have the chance to test, compare, and think through our ideas with other people. Share your ideas and look for ways to make them stronger whenever your teacher gives you opportunities to talk with a partner, in small groups, or as a whole class.
Show what you know.	A good response will show that you understand the relevant material from the unit. Before developing your response, look back on your learning. What's important to include in your response? How you can organize your ideas to make your response clear?

Window Notes

What is it?

A tool that encourages students to use their notes to ask questions, make connections, and explore their personal feelings (in addition to recording facts)

What are the benefits of using this tool?

The ability to take notes is essential to student success. But most students (and most adults) associate notes with boredom, with mindless copying, with things antithetical to curiosity. Window Notes is a note-taking technique that encourages students to unleash their curiosity on the content they are learning about. With Window Notes, students do more than capture information; they can ask questions, make interesting connections, and express their personal feelings and reactions. Not only does this dynamic approach to notes keep student curiosity at the center of learning, it also engages students in the kind of active processing of content that leads to deep understanding.

What are the basic steps?

1. Tell students that you want them to be more curious note takers by generating notes that capture (1) facts, (2) questions, (3) feelings & reactions, and (4) connections that come to mind.

   Tip: Encourage students to record *any* connections that come to mind—for example, personal, real-world, literary, historical, or academic (i.e., connections to things they've learned in school).

2. Review the Window Notes organizer (p. 61) with students. Show them how it has a place for each of the four note types mentioned in Step 1, as well as guiding questions to spur their thinking.

3. Model the Window Notes process for students. Select a topic or text, and make all four types of notes about that topic or text on the organizer. Think aloud as you work. Let your curiosity show!

4. Ask students to generate Window Notes about a specific topic, text, lecture, or other classroom presentation. They can use the Window Notes organizer on p. 61, make their own organizers, or express their thoughts orally (ideal for younger students).

   Tip: Before having students create content-related Window Notes, let them practice making Window Notes about a topic that's very familiar to them (e.g., a day in their life). Observe students as they work, and provide guidance or feedback as needed.

5. Invite students to share their notes with the class. Review key ideas and address students' questions if appropriate. Instruct students to add to or revise their notes as they see fit.

6. Encourage students to use the Window Notes technique independently, as a means of making the note-taking process more active, engaging, and personally meaningful. Facilitate the process by making blank Window Notes organizers readily available.

How is this tool used in the classroom?

✔ To promote note taking that includes facts, questions, feelings/reactions, and connections

✔ To make the note-taking process an active, engaging, and personally meaningful one

EXAMPLE 1: Elementary science

After fourth graders read a passage on penguins, their teacher challenged them to work in teams of four to create a set of collaborative Window Notes. Team members shared and discussed their ideas and then worked together to create their notes. One team's Window Notes appear below.

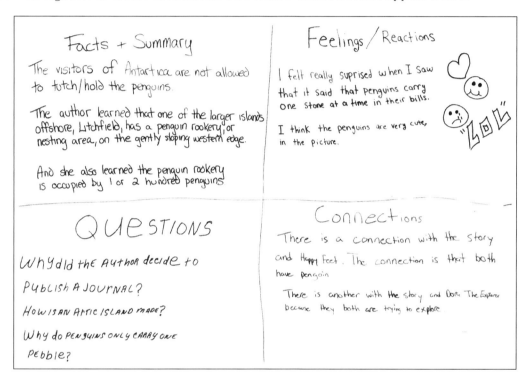

Facts + Summary

The visitors of Antartica are not allowed to tutch/hold the penguins.

The author learned that one of the larger islands offshore, Litchfield, has a penguin rookery, or nesting area, on the gently sloping western edge.

And she also learned the penguin rookery is occupied by 1 or 2 hundred penguins.

Feelings / Reactions

I felt really suprised when I saw that it said that penguins carry one stone at a time in their bills.

I think the penguins are very cute, in the picture.

"LOL"

QUESTIONS

Why did the Author decide to publish a journal?

How is an Artic island made?

Why do penguins only carry one pebble?

Connections

There is a connection with the story and Happy Feet. The connection is that both have penguin

There is another with the story and Dora The Explorer because they both are trying to explore.

EXAMPLE 2: Secondary ELA

A high school student's notes from Maya Angelou's "Caged Bird" are shown below.

FACTS	FEELINGS & REACTIONS
• The poem goes back and forth between a free bird and a caged bird. • The free bird leaps and floats and flies and "claims the sky." • The caged bird's wings are clipped, and its feet are tired. • The poem is written in free verse.	The poem makes me feel sorry for the caged bird. It can't fly and longs to be free. I really like the way it repeats the verse about the caged bird singing of freedom. The song can't be stopped.
QUESTIONS	**CONNECTIONS**
Is the caged bird actually triumphant at the end?	The poem reminds me of a technique they sometimes use in movies where they keep cutting back and forth between two different characters.

EXAMPLE 3: Elementary science

Below are the notes a fourth-grade student made while watching a video on tornadoes.

FACTS	FEELINGS & REACTIONS
• Tornadoes are rotating columns of air. They go from a thunderstorm in the sky down to the ground. • They form when warm moist air hits cool dry air. • They can reach wind speeds of 300 miles per hour.	• Tornadoes are really scary! I didn't know how much damage they could cause!
QUESTIONS	**CONNECTIONS**
• How do they measure the wind speed inside a tornado? • Why don't tornadoes keep going? What makes them stop?	• I saw something about a tornado on TV when my parents were watching the news. Some of the people were crying because their houses had gotten blown away. • Tornadoes remind me of getting off to school. I am trying to do so many things and I am so rushed that it feels like I am spinning at 300 miles per hour!

🎯 Teacher Talk

→ Because many students aren't used to being asked how they feel, particularly in a note-taking context, you may need to spend more time modeling and discussing what goes in the Feelings & Reactions quadrant of the organizer. One way to help is to give students a list of feeling stems that might help them—for example, "I really enjoyed ___," "I was impressed by ___," "I was surprised that ___," "I was inspired by ___," "I was confused about ___," or "I'm not sure how I feel about ___."

→ While this tool is typically used to have students take notes on one specific text or presentation, it can also be used to help students reflect on and demonstrate what they've learned at the end of a lesson sequence or unit. When used in this way, students' completed organizers serve as a great tool for assessing students' learning, interests, open questions, and feelings about the topic or text.

→ Help yourself (and your students) recognize that people can be curious in different ways by surveying the class to see which of the four note types is each student's favorite. Explain that it's fine to have preferences, but that each note type has value—and, therefore, that students should aim to generate all four types of notes, even if some come less naturally to them.

→ Help students appreciate—and encourage them to use—the Window Notes technique by identifying (or challenging them to identify) the value of each note type. Among other things, you might note that recording FACTS helps students extract and summarize key content, generating QUESTIONS invites students to wonder about the contents, expressing FEELINGS & REACTIONS lets students connect with what they're learning on a personal level, and making CONNECTIONS encourages students to tap into their prior knowledge.

→ Some teachers may wonder if this technique is "fluffy." But, in reality, it promotes deeper understanding than traditional note taking. Why? Because making the four types of notes requires active processing and ensures that students are not simply copying, which can be done mindlessly.

Name: _____   Date: _____

Topic or text: _____

Window Notes

FACTS What did you learn?	FEELINGS & REACTIONS How did you feel about what you saw, heard, or read?
QUESTIONS What do you want to know or wonder about?	CONNECTIONS Can you make any connections to people, places, or things you know about? Or to experiences you've had?

Creating an Inner Fire

I think, at a child's birth, if a mother could ask a fairy godmother to endow it with the most useful gift, that gift should be curiosity.

—Eleanor Roosevelt

All theories agree that curiosity's immediate function is to learn, explore, and immerse oneself in the interesting event. In the long term, curiosity serves a broader function of building knowledge and competence. Exploring new events fosters learning new things, meeting new people, and developing new skills.

—Todd B. Kashdan and Paul J. Silvia,
"Curiosity and Interest: The Benefits of Thriving on Novelty and Challenge"

As teachers, our goal is to stop teaching.

Now, now … that's not as cynical as it sounds. We merely mean that the purpose of teaching isn't simply to *teach*, but rather to help students *learn*—and to show them how to learn on their own, even when there's no teacher around. At some point, if we're successful, students will be able to guide their own learning, and we can step back as the central figure in their education. We become, as the adage goes, a guide on the side rather than a sage on the stage.

But first, let's take stock of where we are. Let's suppose at this point, you have been successful in getting students more excited about learning (sparking curiosity) and keeping them actively engaged so that their learning becomes deep (fanning the flame). This is no small feat. You've captured and sustained curiosity to help students learn something well.

Yet there's something else—something even more powerful—you can help nurture in students. It's a deeper form of curiosity that goes beyond the spark of curiosity and the flame of ongoing interest and thinking. It's something researchers call *trait curiosity*—a habit of mind, an inner drive that develops as we begin to embrace curiosity thinking (Loewenstein, 1994). In short, it's a fire that builds inside us when we go beyond simply *feeling* curious and start *being* curious.

The tools in this chapter will help you nurture students' inner curiosity so that students begin to *see themselves as curious*. These tools invite students to ask and seek answers to their own questions, establish and achieve learning goals born out of their natural curiosity, and transfer what they learn in the classroom to real-world contexts. By integrating these tools into your teaching, you'll help your students turn the sparks and flames of curiosity into that self-sustaining fire inside. And with that fire fully kindled inside them—with the curiosity habit fully formed—students will be better able to pursue deep learning, explore the world around them, and achieve self-actualization.

The eight tools for creating this inner fire in students are as follows:

1. **Claim Check** helps students develop a "curious, but critical" mindset by teaching them to investigate the validity of claims they encounter in texts and the media.

2. **Curiosity Cards** empowers students to develop and pursue personal learning goals based on what interests or intrigues them.

3. **Curiosity Clubs** invites students to work with fellow learners to learn more about topics of common interest.

4. **Curiosity Stems** provides simple, ready-to-use sentence starters that help students get in the habit of identifying and articulating what they're especially curious about.

5. **From Puzzles to Paradoxes** gives teachers a set of frameworks for designing tasks that increase motivation and engage students in real-world thinking.

6. **GRASPS** helps teachers design "from-scratch" tasks that capture students' attention, incorporate real-world elements, and promote the transfer of learning to new contexts.

7. **Observe, Describe, Question** helps students develop the curiosity skills of observation (so they notice more about the world around them) and questioning (so they can turn their observations into questions that fuel learning).

8. **The Write Way to Motivate** makes classroom writing exciting by replacing run-of-the-mill writing tasks with tasks that invite creativity, discovery, and personal expression.

Claim Check

What is it?

A tool that teaches students to question and investigate the validity of claims they encounter on television, on the Internet, in print, and elsewhere

What are the benefits of using this tool?

In *Out of Curiosity*, author Bryan Goodwin (2018) cautions that we may be becoming the "land of the easily duped" (p. 138) as our collective curiosity—our capacity to question and think things through—seems to be waning with the ascent of social media echo chambers and political groupthink. Thus, it is more important than ever to teach students how to avoid being duped by the many and often misleading claims found in today's environment. Claim Check teaches students how to investigate the validity of the claims they come across online, in the media, and elsewhere. It also helps students curtail impulsivity and develop a questioning attitude—habits of mind that Costa and Kallick (2008) have found are characteristic of good thinkers.

What are the basic steps?

1. Talk to students about the importance of evaluating the claims they encounter on TV, in texts, etc.

2. Present students with a specific claim to evaluate. For example:

- How valid is the claim that first grade is more challenging than kindergarten?
- How valid is this person's claim that children your age need ten hours of sleep per night?
- How valid is this organization's claim that vaccines cause autism?
- How valid is this advertisement's claim that chili pepper extract can help you lose weight?
- How valid is this article's claim that music education promotes broader academic success?
- How valid is this writer's claim that texting and driving is more dangerous than driving drunk?
- How valid is the congressman's claim that human activities contribute to global warming?
- How valid is the claim that weight lifting is a better weight-loss strategy than aerobic exercise?

3. Have students search for evidence for/against the given claim and make an informed judgment about the claim's validity. Train students to consider the soundness, relevance, and sufficiency of the evidence they find (as well as the credibility of their sources) when making their judgments.

Tip: Prepare students to be successful by modeling the process of gathering and evaluating evidence. Evaluate several claims as a class before asking students to check any on their own.

4. Ask students to explain what they decided and why. ("This claim appears to be valid because…" or "I question this claim because I found two reputable sources that contradict it.")

5. Review students' reasoning. If needed, use probing questions to help students clarify, expand, or re-evaluate their thinking. ("Should a celebrity's beliefs on this issue outweigh concrete data from the medical research community?" "Did you verify that information using multiple sources?")

6. Encourage students to check claims independently—not just when you tell them to, and not just in school, but always. ("Don't believe everything you read or hear. Check the evidence!")

How is this tool used in the classroom?

✔ To help students develop a "curious and critical" mindset

✔ To empower students to think critically about claims they encounter

🌑 Teacher Talk

➔ Simplify the tool as needed when using it with younger students, struggling students, or students who are just learning to evaluate claims and evidence. Here are some possible options:

- Instead of using complex claims that require investigation, give students simple statements that are easily checkable and objectively right or wrong (e.g., "All birds can fly").

- Have students evaluate claims as a class or in groups rather than on their own.

- Provide students with sources to consult ("Look for evidence in the books and articles on the back table") rather than having them search for sources on their own. Sources that don't require reading (e.g., videos, graphs, books read aloud) are ideal for very young students and struggling readers.

- Simplify the guidelines for evaluating evidence (Step 3). Instead of requiring students to consider the credibility of their sources, for example, let them use any sources they want.

➔ Talk to students about the potential value of consulting multiple sources when checking a claim.

➔ Help students appreciate the importance of evaluating things they see and hear (on TV, for example) by showing them examples of claims that *aren't* well supported by quality evidence. One option is to have them explore a fact-checking website like the Pulitzer Prize–winning PolitiFact (www.politifact.com).

➔ Use this tool to initiate a conversation about the ways that people's personal biases, points of view, or purposes might affect the claims they make or the evidence they use to support those claims. Point out that the selective use of evidence (i.e., highlighting evidence that supports a claim while ignoring contradictory evidence) is actually a very common phenomenon.

➔ Use concrete examples like those below to help students recognize that searching for evidence doesn't always have to involve doing library-type research—it can involve carrying out experiments, making models, and/or performing calculations.

Example: Students could check the claim that the kitchen sink is the germiest spot in a typical house by *carrying out an experiment.*

Example: Students could *perform some simple calculations* to check the claim that over two billion gallons of water could be saved per year in the United States if people turned the water off while brushing their teeth.

➔ Claim Check supports a number of college and career readiness standards across the content, including those that call for students to evaluate the soundness of arguments and claims; research specific questions, assess the credibility of their sources, and synthesize their findings; and support conclusions with source-based evidence.

Curiosity Cards

What is it?

A tool that encourages students to establish and pursue curiosity-driven learning goals and appreciate the way that curiosity enhances learning

What are the benefits of using this tool?

Successful learners tend to be driven by their own curiosity: They notice what interests them, pursue learning related to their interests, and reflect on what they've learned and what they're still curious about. This tool gives teachers a powerful technique (in the form of a tangible Curiosity Card) for nurturing this kind of curiosity-driven learning in all students. It also develops students' self-direction by teaching students how to turn what interests them into clear learning goals and build plans to achieve those goals.

What are the basic steps?

1. Set aside "curiosity time" for students to focus on what they're curious about. You may want to use the Curiosity Stems tool on p. 72 to help students identify areas of interest.

2. Have students establish a learning goal based on their curiosity and record it on a Curiosity Card. Choose one of the two Curiosity Card formats on p. 69, or allow students to create their own.

3. Meet with students one-on-one to discuss their goals and help them develop plans for achieving their goals. Once a solid plan has been agreed upon, sign—and have students sign—their Curiosity Card.

 Tip: Talk to students about different ways they might want to share their findings, either with you or with the class.

4. Help students execute their plans, monitor their progress, and adjust their plans as needed. One simple way to help students execute and monitor their plans is to have them check off each step in their plan as it is completed, as shown in Example 2.

5. Call attention to ways in which students' curiosity and corresponding actions influence their success. ("You were eager to learn about teens' use of social media, which led to your decision to conduct personal interviews. Those interviews yielded some eye-opening information!")

6. Use questions like these to help students reflect on what they learned and the impact that their curiosity had on their learning:

- What did you learn as a result of this process?
- How did pursuing your own curiosity affect your motivation to learn? How did it affect how much effort you gave? How did it affect the degree to which you enjoyed doing the work?
- What did you learn from this process that could help you be more successful in school and beyond school?
- What are you still curious about?

How is this tool used in the classroom?

✔ To help students pursue their curiosity in the classroom

✔ To build students' self-direction as learners

✔ To help students appreciate the way curiosity enhances learning

EXAMPLE 1: Elementary social studies

During a unit on his local community, a third-grade student became interested in learning about his grandfather's community in Nigeria. He developed the Curiosity Card below as a result.

This Curiosity Card belongs to *Habib Adebayo*

Goal: *I want to learn about the community in Nigeria that Grandpa grew up in. I want to know how it is like my community and how it is different.*

Date goal established: *January 24th*   **Date goal achieved:**

Action plan: *I will interview Grandpa on FaceTime. I will ask him questions like "What was school like? Were there grocery and toy stores? Were there playgrounds and libraries?" Ms. Rojas will help me find books on growing up in Nigeria. I also talked to Ms. Rojas about how I can share what I learn with the class. I think I will make a flipbook that shows how my community and Grandpa's community are similar and how they are different.*

Student signature: *Habib Adebayo*   **Teacher signature:** *Ms. Rojas*

EXAMPLE 2: Secondary science

While learning about human body systems, a middle school student became curious about how doctors and scientists from the past figured out what internal body systems look like and how they work. Her Curiosity Card appears below.

This Curiosity Card belongs to *Celia Thomas*   **Date:** *November 2nd*   **Subject:** *Science*

What I'm curious about: *I am curious about how doctors and scientists figured out what the body systems looked like and how they functioned before there were X-rays and MRIs. How did they figure these things out?*

My goal: *To learn how doctors and scientists from the past learned about the internal systems of the human body.*

Action plan (✓off each step that you accomplish):   **Completion Date:**

☑ 1 *I will conduct some library and Internet research to get the "lay of the land."*   *November 12th*

☑ 2 *I will decide on a few key people or breakthroughs to focus on.*   *November 18th*

☐ 3 *I will develop a simple timeline to highlight important people and events.*

Basic Curiosity Card

This Curiosity Card belongs to_____

Start date: _____ Achievement date: _____

My goal is to

Here is what I will do to try and achieve my goal:

Curiosity Card with Checklist

This Curiosity Card belongs to_____ Date: _____

What I'm curious about:

My goal:

Action plan (✓ off each step that you accomplish and record the completion date): | Completion date:

☐ 1

☐ 2

☐ 3

☐ 4

☐ 5

☐ 6

Student signature: Teacher signature:

Curiosity Clubs

What is it?

A tool that empowers students to learn more about aspects of the content they're curious about and pursue their learning with fellow students who share similar interests

What are the benefits of using this tool?

One way to help students develop trait curiosity, or the "fire inside to keep learning" (Goodwin, Gibson, Lewis, & Rouleau, 2018, p. 71) is to remember the power of the club. After all, book clubs, cooking clubs, film clubs, etc. are great examples of people who pursue learning passionately and continuously. But why do people join clubs in the first place? Two words: *choice* and *community*. Club members choose their clubs based on what's interesting to them, and they learn with the support and nourishment of a community of fellow learners. Curiosity Clubs is designed to help teachers put these same guiding principles to work in the classroom. It helps students discover particular areas of interest within the curriculum, and it empowers students to work in small groups to explore and learn more about their interests.

What are the basic steps?

1. Tell students that they will have the opportunity to choose an aspect of the content that interests them and explore it in greater depth with a group of classmates who share that same interest.

2. Present students with a choice of texts to read, topics to investigate, activities/experiments to complete, or problems to solve. (To help students discover the qualities of a good friend, for example, you might present them with a choice of classic friendship stories to read.)

   Note: The idea isn't just to give students choices; it's to give them choices that will help them achieve a specific learning goal (for example, identifying the qualities of a good friend).

3. Allow students to sample the different options (e.g., by skimming the first page of each text or reading a brief description of the different topics) and choose the one that interests them most.

   Tip: You can gain insight into students' interests and expose students to other perspectives by inviting students to discuss their choices as a class. Ask questions like, "Why does this interest you? Why did you choose this and not that? Does anyone want to change his/her initial choice?"

4. Establish Curiosity Clubs by having students meet up with classmates who made the same choice.

5. Explain what each club is expected to do, learn, or produce. ("Find information or examples in the story that will help you define what it means to be a good friend.") Check in periodically to be sure that all students are contributing and to provide assistance if needed.

6. Invite each club to share its findings with the class. ("What did your stories teach you about the qualities of a true friend? Let's combine everyone's ideas to create a list of good-friend attributes.")

7. *Optional:* Ask students to apply their learning to a new task. ("Use what you learned to help you decide whether the main character in the story we're about to read is a true friend and why.")

How is this tool used in the classroom?

✔ To nourish and develop students' inner curiosity through choice and collaboration

✔ To empower students to explore particular aspects of the content in greater depth

There are many ways to establish Curiosity Clubs in the classroom. One of the simplest is to let students choose a text that they're interested in reading, as shown in the "friendship" example that's embedded in the steps on the previous page. Other options are highlighted below.

EXAMPLE 1: Give students a choice of source types/media to explore

A high school teacher challenged students to develop their understanding of the current debate over immigration policy by examining and extracting as much information as they could from whichever one of the following sources they were most interested in exploring: newspaper editorial, data chart, personal account, or series of political cartoons.

EXAMPLE 2: Give students a choice of real-world applications to investigate

A middle school math teacher presented students with a list of ways that people in different fields use linear equations in the real world: "Trainers and sports teams use linear equations to analyze athletic performance," "Business and sales teams use linear equations to evaluate sales and make projections," etc. Students chose the field they were most curious about and worked in Curiosity Clubs to learn the specifics of how linear equations are used by people in their selected field.

EXAMPLE 3: Allow students to explore the content from different angles or perspectives

A history teacher uses Curiosity Clubs as a means of helping students explore historical events from multiple perspectives (a goal of her curriculum standards). During a unit on westward expansion, for example, she invites students to explore how westward expansion affected one of the following groups: Native Americans, settlers, entrepreneurs, women, or children.

EXAMPLE 4: Set up different experiments or activities to help students learn about a topic

To help students develop their understanding of gravity, a science teacher let them choose whether they wanted to (1) create a simple "gravity device" using a candle, needle, and cups; (2) mimic Galileo's famous experiment by dropping balls of different sizes, weights, and materials and tracking the results; (3) experiment with inclined planes; or (4) use a computer simulation to test the effects of different variables on gravitational force.

EXAMPLE 5: Encourage students to explore a specific example of a larger topic/theme

An art history teacher set up an in-class art gallery featuring multiple examples of modern art. She instructed students to walk through the gallery, "find a piece that really speaks to you," and then research both the piece and the artist who composed it with classmates who had been drawn to the same piece that they had.

Curiosity Stems

What is it?

A simple way to get students in the "curiosity habit"—the regular practice of wondering, asking questions, reflecting, and seeking new learning

What are the benefits of using this tool?

One of the great paradoxes of school is that what should serve to incubate students' curiosity often suffocates it instead. Indeed, research shows that many students spend their entire school day "without asking even one question or engaging in one sequence of behavior aimed at finding out something new" (Engel, 2011, p. 633). That's obviously the bad news. The good news is that changing this dynamic need not be difficult. Curiosity stems are simple thought-starters that invite students to exercise their curiosity regularly. Teachers can use the stems at the beginning of instruction to get students excited about learning, throughout instruction to help students explore ideas, and at the end of instruction to encourage students to reflect on and continue their learning. By using the stems regularly, teachers help students get used to thinking curiously, so that the acts of wondering, questioning, and actively pursuing new learning can become lifelong habits.

What are the basic steps?

1. Set aside "curiosity time" at key points throughout an instructional sequence.

2. Invite students to get curious about their learning by completing one of the curiosity stems below. Depending on your goals and where you are in the lesson sequence, you might select particular stems, or you might allow students to choose which stem they would like to use.

I wonder . . .	*What would it be like to . . .*	*I am fascinated with . . .*
What if . . .	*I am perplexed by . . .*	*I can imagine . . .*
I want to know more about . . .	*Why . . .*	*I am intrigued by . . .*
How is it possible that . . .	*How the heck does ___ work?*	*I might want to try . . .*
What is the evidence for . . .	*I am curious about why . . .*	*Is it really the case that . . .*

3. Invite students to share their responses, either in small groups or as a class.

4. Use students' responses as a springboard to promote new learning. Address areas of interest in future lessons, and encourage students to pursue and report on their interests independently by establishing curiosity journals or boards where they can post their completed stems and findings.

5. Explain that curiosity is a key to success in school and life. Help students build the curiosity habit by using the tool regularly and by being a "curiosity model" (i.e., stop regularly during instruction and use a curiosity stem to express your own curiosity about the topic under investigation).

How is this tool used in the classroom?

✔ To get students in the regular habit of expressing and pursuing their curiosity

From Puzzles to Paradoxes

What is it?

A tool for designing assessment tasks that increase students' learning drive by actively engaging students in real-world thinking and reasoning

What are the benefits of using this tool?

When it comes to designing assessment tasks, here's an important but under-asked question: What kinds of real-world tasks and thinking challenges actually capture people's attention and inspire their effort? From Puzzles to Paradoxes was designed with this question in mind. It outlines twelve task-design frameworks that challenge students to apply real-world thinking skills to create a product, solve a problem, or achieve a goal. It also provides simple steps and classroom examples for each framework to help you create high-quality tasks in your own classroom—tasks that are far more likely than traditional tests to engage students in deeper learning and increase their drive to work hard.

What are the basic steps?

1. Identify the content knowledge / thinking skills that you want to develop or assess.

2. Familiarize yourself with the twelve different task-design frameworks. Select a framework that meets your needs.

Note: Guidelines for picking a framework can be found on p. 74; detailed descriptions, instructions, and examples can be found on pp. 75–77.

3. Use your selected framework to create an assessment task for your lesson or unit. Ask yourself the following questions as you develop your task:

- *What* do I want students to produce? (An argument essay? A verbal explanation? A poster?)
- *Why* am I assigning this task? Is the task consistent with my goals and purpose?
- *When* and *where* should students work on it? (During instruction or after? In class or at home?)
- *How* should students work on it? (Alone? In pairs? In groups?)
- *What* criteria will I consider when assessing students' work?

4. Present the task to students. Clarify what the task entails, how students should work on it, and how students' work will be evaluated.

How is this tool used in the classroom?

✔ To increase student engagement using authentic types of assessment tasks
✔ To develop and assess students' research, writing, and analytical thinking skills

Which Assessment Framework Should I Choose?

Select the **Puzzle** framework to have students demonstrate their content knowledge and reasoning skills by solving a puzzle or logic problem.

Choose the **Mystery** framework to engage students in developing evidence-based explanations of content-related mysteries or discrepant events.

Use the **Historical Investigation** framework to deepen and test students' understanding of historically significant people, places, and events—and to develop critical research, writing, and thinking skills.

Use the **Controversy** framework to test students' understanding of a controversial issue and ability to support a position with evidence.

Use the **Personal Dilemma** framework to broaden students' perspectives on controversial issues, help students connect with the content on a personal level, and have students express and defend their personal positions.

Use the **Problem/Solution** framework to test students' ability to analyze problems (real-world or fictional), generate solutions, and evaluate the quality of those solutions.

Select the **Invention** framework to have students apply their content knowledge to the creation of an original product.

Select the **Decision-Making** framework to have students make or evaluate decisions using a specific set of criteria.

Use the **Informed Prediction** framework to present students with hypothetical scenarios that require them to understand and apply what they've learned.

Use the **Essential Attributes** framework to test students' understanding of important terms and concepts.

Select the **Experimental Inquiry** framework to assess students' ability to generate and/or test original hypotheses.

Choose the **Paradox** framework to boost engagement and test students' understanding of critical concepts by challenging students to explain seemingly contradictory statements or observations.

From Puzzles to Paradoxes: Twelve Assessment Frameworks to Choose From

FRAMEWORK	TO CREATE THIS KIND OF TASK…	CLASSROOM EXAMPLES
Puzzle Tasks require students to solve or put the pieces of a puzzle together in a logical way.	1. Break a text, process, system, or piece of equipment into parts. 2. Present the parts to students. 3. Challenge students to reconstruct the original and explain their reasoning. *Variation:* Give students *any* logic/reasoning problem to solve.	• Can you arrange these pictures to tell a story? • Can you put the steps in this scrambled geometric proof into a logical order? • A copy of Bertrand Russell's "What I Have Lived For" was recently given to us, but the pieces were all out of order. Use what you know about the power of a thesis statement to drive the organization of an essay, the structure of an essay in general, and the function of transitional words to put the pieces back in order. Justify your organization in writing.
Mystery Tasks challenge students to solve content-related mysteries by analyzing and synthesizing a set of clues.	1. Present a puzzling event/phenomenon ("mystery") to students. 2. Give students a set of clues (facts, maps, data tables, images, etc.) that will help them solve the mystery. 3. Encourage students to review the clues carefully, generate plausible solutions, and select the best one. They can do this alone, in pairs, or in groups of three to five students. 4. Have students present and support their solution with evidence.	• After dominating the earth for over 150 million years, the dinosaurs suddenly disappeared. Can you figure out why? Generate a hypothesis that is consistent with the bits of information ("clues") in your team's envelope. Be prepared to justify your hypothesis. • Over the course of twenty years, more than 80% of the people who settled in Jamestown died. Why might this be? Look for clues in your textbook. Propose an explanation. • A kindergarten mystery: "I live in a den and can roar very loud. In the jungle, I am king—and of that I am proud! Who am I?"
Historical Investigations ask students to research, analyze, and draw conclusions about historically significant events.	1. Choose a historically significant event for students to research and explore, either individually or as a class. 2. Pose a question that requires them to think about the event in an analytical way (e.g., What were its causes? Its effects? How does it compare to another event? Why is it significant?). 3. Have students present the results of their analysis. *Variation:* Move beyond events. Have students research historically significant people, discoveries, works of literature, and so on.	• Why do athletes from around the world compete in the Olympics every four years? How did this tradition get started? Do the Olympics still matter today? Why? • How did the Space Race affect our country's spending priorities, schools, and achievements? • Were there any silver linings in the sinking of the RMS *Titanic*? • What was Upton Sinclair's purpose in writing *The Jungle*? Did the book have its intended effect? • Can a disease alter the course of world history? Explain using one or more of the examples on the board.
Controversy Tasks have students take and defend a position on a debatable or unresolved issue.	1. Identify an issue that people have different theories/positions on. 2. Pose a question that will get students thinking about that issue. 3. Challenge students to research/consider all sides of the issue, take a position, and justify their position using evidence. If appropriate, have them mention and rebut alternative positions. *Note:* For controversies that revolve around personal values, morals, or feelings, use the Personal Dilemma framework instead.	• Should members of Congress have term limits? • Does "fairness" mean treating everyone the same? • What was President Lincoln's primary motive in signing the Emancipation Proclamation? • Does Pythagoras deserve the credit for the theorem that's named after him? • What's the best way to stimulate the economy during a recession? • Do street artists deserve to be studied alongside art giants like Picasso and Matisse?

(continued on next page)

From Puzzles to Paradoxes: Twelve Assessment Frameworks to Choose From (continued)

FRAMEWORK	TO CREATE THIS KIND OF TASK…	CLASSROOM EXAMPLES
Personal Dilemma Tasks are similar to Controversy tasks in that they require taking a position on a controversial issue, but they place more emphasis on personal feelings/values.	1. Identify an issue that students will have different views about. 2. Pose a question that requires students to take a position on this issue. (Dilemma questions often start with the word *should*.) 3. Have students present and defend their positions. 4. Clarify that a well-crafted response should reflect factual knowledge as well as feelings; it should also mention the positives and negatives of taking that particular position.	• Should our constitutionally given right to free speech be limited under any circumstances? • Should professional female athletes earn the same as their male counterparts? • Should we be nice to people even when they're not nice to us? • Should a top-notch education include instruction in art and music? • Should animals be used in scientific research? • Should George have shot Lennie at the end of *Of Mice and Men*?
Problem/Solution Tasks ask students to analyze a problem, generate possible solutions, and evaluate those solutions.	1. Present students with a content-related problem or challenge that could be addressed in a variety of ways. 2. Have them analyze the problem, generate possible solutions, and select the best one. (This can be done individually or in groups.) *Variation:* Have students examine and evaluate someone else's solution to a problem.	• How might we get the students in this school to care more about recycling? • Can you think of a way to help Frog and Toad solve their cookie-eating problem? [A teacher posed this question after reading part of Arnold Lobel's "Cookies" aloud.] • How could we increase the strength of this paper tube? Explain and support your ideas. • How could we address the issue of low voter turnout? • How effectively did George Washington address the morale problem among his troops?
Invention Tasks challenge students to create or invent an original product.	1. Challenge students to create or invent something that solves a problem, fulfills a need, or improves an existing product/design. 2. Encourage them to be creative yet practical and think outside the box. *Note:* This framework differs from Problem/Solution in that it requires students to create something concrete—for example, a drawing or a product rather than an idea or strategy.	• Invent a "study diet" that could improve students' academic performance. • Create a fun name for a healthy snack that would get students more interested in eating it (e.g., "ants on a log" instead of "celery with cream cheese and raisins"). • Invent a fitness routine that people could do in their hotel rooms without any equipment. • The local zoo has hired you to redesign the enclosure for an animal of your choice. The new enclosure should promote the health and happiness of your animal while providing maximum visibility and entertainment for zoo visitors.
Decision-Making Tasks require students to analyze different options, pick one, and defend their choice.	1. Pose a question that requires students to consider alternatives and make a decision. For example, "Who/what is the best ___?" 2. Tell students what criteria they should use to analyze the various alternatives or let them choose their own criteria. 3. Ask students to explain and defend their decisions. (What did I decide? How did the criteria guide my decision-making process?) *Variation:* Have students use specific criteria to evaluate someone else's decision (e.g., a politician's or literary character's).	• Imagine that you meet people from another planet who don't know what *friendship* is. Which book from this unit would you pick to help them understand what it is? Why? • Who was the most influential ruler of ancient Egypt? Defend your choice. • If you were the coach, what play would you call in this situation? Why? • Do you agree that bombing Hiroshima and Nagasaki was President Truman's best option for ending the war in the Pacific? Use the criteria on the board to compare the options that were available to Truman and decide what you would've done if you were president. Present, explain, and defend your decision in a letter to the American people.

Task Type	Steps	Examples
Informed Prediction Tasks present students with a "what if" scenario and ask them to generate possible outcomes.	1. Present students with a "what if" scenario. 2. Have them describe possible outcomes (or causes). 3. Make it clear that their predictions should be rooted in their knowledge of the subject matter (i.e., predictions should be logical, not nonsensical).	• What if we had a base-60 number system like the ancient Babylonians instead of base-10? • What if there weren't any oil in the Middle East? • What if the sun stopped shining? • What if Rasputin had never lived? • What if you traveled into the future and found that the United States was no longer the superpower it is today? What might have caused this change in status?
Essential Attributes Tasks challenge students to recognize, apply, or define a key concept's essential attributes.	1. Select a critical concept that students have learned about. 2. Test students' understanding of this concept by assigning a task that requires them to recognize, apply, or define its essential attributes/elements. Among other things, you could have students find real-world examples of the concept, list its critical attributes, or explain how it's similar to or different from another concept.	• Show that you understand the key elements of a fable by writing one of your own. • What is an amphipathic molecule? Define it in your own words, draw a real-world example of one, and use the drawing to highlight its essential attributes/parts. • The Notre Dame Cathedral is considered a classic example of Gothic architecture. Why? • Is Willy Loman a true tragic hero? Defend your position using evidence from the text. • What is a rational number? How does it differ from an irrational number?
Experimental Inquiries challenge students to generate and test original hypotheses.	1. Ask students to make an educated guess about the outcome of an action, event, or experiment. 2. Have them generate a plan for testing their guess. 3. Whenever possible, have them carry out their plans and report their results.	• If you were a plant, do you think the kind of light you got would matter (artificial vs. sunlight)? How could you test your prediction? Let's design an experiment to find out. … • How might using fewer lectures and more hands-on activities affect learning, motivation, and/or engagement? Make a prediction and explain how we could test it as a class. • How might adding resistors affect the current in a series circuit? Make a prediction, generate a plan for testing it, and describe the results of your experiment.
Paradox Tasks challenge students to explain seemingly contradictory statements or observations.	1. Present students with a seemingly contradictory statement or phenomenon that is nonetheless true. ("How is it possible that _?") 2. Challenge students to reconcile the paradox by generating possible explanations.	How is it possible that … • Eating fewer calories can actually prevent you from losing weight? • George Washington lost more battles than he won, yet is one of our greatest war heroes? • Airplanes are extremely heavy but don't fall out of the sky? • The order of operations can affect your answer? • Burning a forest can be good for its health?

🌀 Teacher Talk

→ Feel free to use the twelve frameworks for instructional purposes as well as assessment purposes (i.e., to help students learn about a topic or issue rather than to test their understanding of it).

→ Can these frameworks be used with very young students? Absolutely! Primary-grade examples have been provided for most of the given frameworks, and the frameworks can be simplified as needed for use with younger students. Among other things, you could have primary-grade students draw or speak their ideas/findings rather than write them.

→ Giving students choices about their learning can enhance their motivation and success. One option is to give students an assessment framework and let them design a task that interests them. Here's how one teacher did this using the Decision-Making framework: "FDR made a lot of important decisions in his first hundred days as president. Pick one that you want to evaluate, describe the criteria that you'll use to do it, and present the results of your analysis in writing." Another option is to use the different frameworks to create a sampler of assessment tasks (see below for an example) and let students choose which task(s) to complete.

ASSESSMENT SAMPLER: Renewable/Nonrenewable Energy Unit (complete *ONE* of these tasks)		
Controversy Is global warming more a result of natural or human causes? Write an editorial taking a position on this issue. Be sure to define global warming, explain the controversy, and defend your position (rebut the alternative one as well) using relevant evidence.	**Investigation** In *Flat, Hot, and Crowded*, Thomas Friedman contends that the more the United States is dependent on oil from the Middle East, the less democratic the Middle East will be. Why does he believe this to be true? Does our reliance on fossil fuels work against the development of democratic principles in the Middle East?	**Informed Prediction** Prepare a presentation in which you use data charts, mathematical calculations, and other evidence to predict the possible consequences if the causes of global warming aren't addressed and temperatures continue to rise at the same rate they've been increasing over the last 100 years.
Controversy + Investigation Research the pros and cons of nuclear energy, natural gas, and solar energy. Conduct a debate on which form of energy should be expanded to meet rising demands for cleaner energy sources.	**Decision Making + Problem/Solution** Select the form of renewable energy that you believe the United States should pursue most aggressively. Identify a challenge in expanding its use and develop a plan that will address this challenge.	**Paradox** Scientists claim that global warming leads to more severe winters and, at the same time, warms the oceans. How is this possible? Explain.

→ Collectively, the assessment frameworks described in this tool engage students in the kinds of higher-order thinking and learning skills that are at the heart of today's college and career readiness standards—for example, analyzing and synthesizing information, evaluating claims and evidence, constructing an argument, and writing for a particular audience.

GRASPS

What is it?

A tool that makes it easy to develop authentic and engaging assessment tasks

What are the benefits of using this tool?

If a hallmark of curious learners is the ability to pursue challenging learning tasks, then we need to give our students regular opportunities to engage in such tasks. This tool, which is based on the work of assessment experts Grant Wiggins and Jay McTighe (2012), makes it easy to design these kinds of tasks. It presents an acronym-based framework for developing rich and authentic tasks that promote learning and are aligned to learning goals and standards. By using this framework to design classroom assessment tasks around intriguing real-world scenarios, we engage students in meaningful work. Just as important, we give them genuine opportunities to become the curious, self-motivated learners we want them to be.

What are the basic steps?

1. Establish the purpose of the performance task you're about to design by asking yourself what standards your task will address, what thinking skills and learning habits your students will practice, and what big ideas / concepts students will need to understand.

2. Design an assessment task that's consistent with your purpose. Make the task authentic and engaging by incorporating real-world elements (see p. 83 for ideas). Use the GRASPS acronym to map out the critical components of the task:

    Goal: What problem, issue, question, or challenge will students tackle? What's the reason or purpose for engaging students in this task?

    Role: What role will students play or persona will they adopt?

    Audience: Who is the target audience that needs to be convinced or informed?

    Situation: What real-world context or setting will draw students in?

    Product/Performance: What kind of product will students create or performance will they give?

    Success criteria: What will you look for in a final product? How will you assess content knowledge / understanding of big ideas? Thinking skills and processes?

3. Use the GRASPS acronym to present the task to students, either at or near the beginning of the unit. Help students analyze the task and think through what it will demand of them. ("If this is our end-product, what will we need to know and be able to do in order to create it?")

4. Empower students to complete the task successfully by ensuring that classroom instruction develops the necessary content knowledge/skills, by modeling the kinds of thinking needed to complete the task, and by reviewing the criteria for success *before* students begin working.

How is this tool used in the classroom?

✔ To craft engaging and authentic assessment tasks

✔ To ensure that assessment tasks are aligned with learning goals and standards

✔ To inspire students' desire to learn and sustain their curiosity

EXAMPLE 1: Primary mathematics

A first-grade teacher used the GRASPS framework to design an assessment task for an upcoming math unit on shapes and their defining attributes. She used her students' fascination with the school's kindergarteners and their excitement about "being the big kids this year" to help her develop a task scenario that she thought would be personally motivating for them. And she ensured that the task was learning focused as well as fun by aligning it to the relevant geometry standards.

Goal:

We are going to help the kindergarten teachers teach their students about shapes.

Role:

Pretend that you are an author. You will work as part of a team to write and illustrate a book for children.

Audience:

Your book will be written for kindergarten students.

Situation:

Our school's kindergarten students need to learn the names and features of many different shapes. The kindergarten teachers are having a hard time finding books to use for their lessons.

Product/Performance:

Your job is to write and illustrate a book that will help the kindergarteners learn what squares, triangles, rectangles, trapezoids, circles, half circles, and quarter circles look like—and what their important features are.

Success criteria:

Here is what you will need to do to create a really great book:

• Draw a picture of each shape.

• Tell what features of each shape are always the same.

• Tell what features can be different.

• Show a picture of each shape from the real world. (We will take a field trip around the school to search for examples, and you can collect more examples at home.)

• Make sure all the pages are pages you are proud of.

EXAMPLE 2: Secondary history

A US history teacher wanted his students to examine and appreciate different groups' perspectives on the American Revolution—specifically, groups whose voices and viewpoints weren't well represented in their course textbook (e.g., women, African Americans, Native Americans, British Loyalists). He used the GRASPS framework to develop a task that he believed would encourage this kind of exploration and empathy.

Goal:

Your goal is to tell the story of the American Revolution in a way that highlights the perspective of a group whose story isn't often told—and to tell it in a way that will promote understanding and empathy.

Role:

You are a filmmaker who has always been fascinated by the American Revolution. You are eager to make a film about the war that showcases the untold story of a group whose story you believe is worth telling. You have started thinking about groups whose stories you might want to tell—women, African Americans, Native Americans, and British Loyalists—but you need to do more research to determine which group's story would make the most compelling film.

Audience:

You ran into a producer who just happened to be negotiating with a major TV studio to produce a limited series of films called *The Untold Stories of America*, and she invited you to pitch your idea for a film at a future meeting.

Situation:

Multiple filmmakers will be pitching their "untold story" ideas to the producer. It's up to you to make sure that your idea gets selected.

Product/Performance:

Your job is to sell your vision to the producer by developing a compelling, well-thought-out, and well-researched film proposal. Your proposal should include an executive summary and a representation of your vision (this can take the form of a written-out scene, storyboard, or short video).

Success criteria:

A clear and compelling proposal should address the *what*, *why*, and *how* of your film. Specifically:

- What is your focus? Which group's story is a story that needs to be told?

- Why do you believe that it's important to share this particular group's story?

- How will you present this group's story in a way that will be compelling for a mass audience and that will encourage empathy on the part of viewers?

EXAMPLE 3: Secondary ELA

A middle school ELA teacher used GRASPS to design a task for an upcoming unit on Greek mythology. The task, which was presented in the form of a letter from a comic book company to make it more authentic and fun, was one that students couldn't wait to get started on! But it was designed to do more than capture their interest, as completing the task well required them to apply both content knowledge from the mythology unit and writing skills that they had been working on in class (e.g., writing narratives with well-developed event sequences, using descriptive language to convey ideas, using visuals to emphasize important details or themes). Notice that while the letter doesn't include the GRASPS acronym explicitly, it does address all the components of the acronym.

Dear seventh-grade students of Pleasant Valley Middle School,

Help! Our staff here at Marvel(ous) Comics is exhausted. Writers are blocked; editors have nothing to edit; illustrators have empty drawing boards. We are pulling our hair out and racking our brains, but we cannot come up with a new superhero for our readers.

Your mission is to create that superhero! We reached out to you because we know that you're getting ready to begin a mythology unit, and we suspect that the characters you'll meet and the adventures they'll embark on will provide great inspiration. We believe that you can use what you'll learn during the unit to help you create a compelling new character that our readers will love.

Your entry will be judged by a panel of writers, illustrators, and publishers (the people who need to be convinced that the character and story will sell). Thus, a successful entry will need to please all of them.

To win over the publishers, you'll need to present your superhero in a compelling way.

- Introduce your hero and describe the world in which he/she lives. Remember that your hero—like the heroes you'll meet in your mythology unit—should have some special talents, skills, or powers.

- Develop your character fully. Describe your hero's talents/skills/powers (make sure they're drawn from at least three of the characters you'll meet in your unit), and explain why they're important in his/her world.

- Use the kind of descriptive language you've been working on in class to make your character come to life.

To win over the writers and illustrators, you'll need to create a storyboard for one of your hero's adventures.

- Impress the writers by incorporating essential "hero-story elements" that you'll learn about during the unit (e.g., a mission/goal/quest, a conflict that must be resolved) and by incorporating the kind of snappy dialogue that you've been learning to develop in class.

- Capture the attention of the illustrators by developing an eye-catching costume that reflects your hero's powers or personality (use the illustrations from the myths you read in class for inspiration) and by using your illustrations to emphasize important ideas or themes.

In addition to the criteria for success outlined above, your entry should (of course!) be proofread, polished, and professional!

Good luck,
Marvel(ous) Comics

Real-World Elements for Making Tasks Authentic

ROLES & AUDIENCES

Activist	Economist	Judge	Pilot
Actor	Editor	Jury	Politician
Advertiser	Enemy	Lawyer	Protestor
Artist	Engineer	Librarian	Rebel
Author	Expert in a specific field	Literary critic	Reporter
Biographer	Explorer	Mathematician	School principal
Blogger	Eyewitness	Mechanic	Scientist
Businessperson	Family member	Meteorologist	Senior citizen
Candidate	Famous athlete	Military leader or veteran	Social worker
Cartoonist	Farmer	Motivational speaker	Sociologist
Chef	Filmmaker	Museum director/Curator	Statistician
Choreographer	Financial planner	Musician	Supreme Court justice
Coach	Firefighter	Newscaster	Teacher
Community leader	Fortune teller	Nutritionist	Textbook publisher
Client/Customer	Friend	Parent	Therapist
Construction worker	Geologist	Passenger/Traveler	TV or radio host
Composer	Grant writer	Peer	Website designer
Dancer	Historian	Pen pal	World leader
Detective	Immigrant	Personal hero	Young child
Disheartened individual	Illustrator	Personal trainer	Yourself
Doctor	Inventor	Photographer	Zookeeper

PRODUCTS & PERFORMANCES

Advertisement	Editorial	Museum display	Questionnaire
Analogy	Essay	Newscast	Recipe
Blog	Family tree	Newspaper article	Report (lab, book, police)
Board game	Flag	Oral presentation	Research report
Brochure	Game	Outline	Scrapbook collage
Bulletin board	Graph/Data display	Painting	Screenplay
Business plan	Graphic organizer	Picture or poster	Script
Case study	Infomercial	Play or puppet show	Sketch or blueprint
Children's book	Instruction manual	Playbook	Slideshow
Computer program	Interview transcript	Podcast	Slogan
Critique	Invention	Poem	Song/Musical performance
Crossword puzzle	Lesson plan	Political cartoon	Speech
Dance	Letter or memo	Portfolio/e-portfolio	Story, myth, or fable
Debate	Map or globe	Position paper/Policy brief	Summary
Demonstration	Memoir	Poster	Textbook section
Diary or journal entry	Metaphor	Problem set & answer key	To-do list
Diet or exercise plan	Model	Proof	Travel brochure
Dramatization	Movie or music video	Proposal	Website/Wiki

CONTEXTS FOR DEVELOPING TASK SITUATIONS

Architecture & design	Current events	Law & criminal justice	Research
Arts & literature	Entertainment	Marketing/Advertising	Science & technology
Communication	Health & medicine	Money & finance	Sociology
Community/Social service	History	Personal history	Sports
Computer science	Industrial arts	Photography	Teaching/Education
Counseling	Invention & manufacturing	Politics & government	Technical writing
Culinary arts	Journalism/Publishing	Radio & television	Travel & tourism

Observe, Describe, Question

What is it?

A technique that encourages students to *observe* carefully, *describe* what they notice, and generate *questions* based on their observations

What are the benefits of using this tool?

Curious learners are constant observers. They pay attention to what's going on around them, and they tend to notice details that others miss. Curious learners are also notorious questioners who are always on the lookout for answers and for new questions to ask. Observe, Describe, Question develops these behaviors in all students. It teaches a three-part thinking process that helps students notice more and generate questions that are interesting to them *and* born out of careful observation.

What are the basic steps?

1. Present students with an item that they will be able to observe closely and generate a wealth of questions about (e.g., an object, animal, data chart, 3-D model, piece of art).

   Note: The tool can also be used to help students carefully examine and ask questions about a learning experience (as shown in Example 2) or a text (as shown in Example 3).

2. Give students dedicated time to OBSERVE/examine the selected item. Encourage them to pay attention to observable details (e.g., features, colors, patterns, discrepancies). Then ask students to DESCRIBE what they observe or notice using words and/or pictures.

3. Ask students to take a second look. Challenge them to find at least one thing that they didn't notice the first time—ideally more!

4. Invite students to share their observations, either in small groups or as a class.

5. Have students review everyone's observations and jot down any QUESTIONS that spring up. (Observing food scattered all over a zoo animal's enclosure might lead students to ask why the food is scattered versus just put out in a single spot.) Clarify that all questions are welcome.

   Tip: To help students develop their question-generating skills, you may want to model and discuss some common types of questions. See Teacher Talk for suggestions.

6. Invite students to share their questions, either in small groups or as a class.

7. *Optional:* Allow students to identify questions that they want to pursue, and work with them to develop a plan for answering those questions. Depending on your goals, students might use their questions to guide research, design an experiment, or develop a design project.

How is this tool used in the classroom?

✔ To help all students develop the behaviors associated with curious learners

✔ To teach students how to observe closely and describe carefully

✔ To invite students to develop questions that are driven by their observations and curiosity

EXAMPLE 1: Primary science

As part of a unit on animals and habitats, a second-grade teacher asks students to OBSERVE the fish and their habitat in the classroom fish tank. Students draw the fish tank and record important details that they notice in their drawings (DESCRIBE). The teacher then encourages students to generate their own QUESTIONS about the fish and fish tank based on their observations. Together, the teacher and students review all of the questions and identify three questions they can investigate as a class. One student's drawing, observations, and questions appear below.

EXAMPLE 2: Career and technical education (CTE)

High school students in the food-service track of their CTE program are having a "learning meal" at a local restaurant. Their teacher uses Observe, Describe, Question to guide their learning in the following way:

- During their meal, students carefully OBSERVE everything they can about what goes into their dining experience. Students make notes to DESCRIBE what they notice.
- After their visit, students share their observations and use the sharing experience to add to and refine their descriptions.
- Working as a class, students use their collective observations to generate QUESTIONS they hope to investigate as they learn more about the restaurant industry.

Some of the students' observations and the questions they generated as a result of their observations are highlighted in the table below.

OBSERVATIONS	QUESTIONS
We were seated near a table of screaming kids, even though there were lots of open tables.	Why were we seated there? What determines where a customer gets seated?
I ordered the fish special but was told that they had run out of it.	How does a restaurant determine how much food to buy (risk of running out vs. spoiling)?
Our server was really attentive.	Are servers trained to check back at certain times?
My french fries were cold and dried out. And my burger was really undercooked.	Is this supposed to happen? Or is someone supposed to check the food before it gets served?
My menu felt sticky.	How often do things like menus get cleaned?
Our long rectangular table made it hard to talk to anyone other than the people right near me.	What if large groups were seated at round tables instead? Is there a reason we didn't see any?
Our entire group's meals came out at the same time.	How do they get all the food to come out at the same time, especially with a big group like ours?
Our server took our orders in her head instead of writing them down.	Why would the restaurant have this system? Doesn't it lead to mistakes or forgetting things?
It was freezing cold when we sat down.	Who makes decisions about things like temperature? What if a customer complains?

EXAMPLE 3: Secondary ELA

A middle school English teacher has adapted Observe, Describe, Question to serve as a close-reading technique. She finds it especially useful when she wants students to notice how authors achieve certain effects. She instructs students to read the text closely and to pay attention to (OBSERVE) any word choices, techniques, or descriptions that stand out for them. After reading, students review their observations and DESCRIBE what they noticed and how it affected them as readers. Finally, students raise and discuss QUESTIONS based on their observations (e.g., Why did the author use such "cool" language to describe such a gruesome crime scene? What effect was the author going for by only showing the aftermath of the crime and not the crime itself?).

🔄 Teacher Talk

→ In *Make Just One Change*, Rothstein and Santana (2011) note the generations-old tradition of "rephrasing student questions … to make the question fit better for teaching and learning purposes" (p. 48). When using Observe, Describe, Question, remember that this tool is about students' interests and students' questions, not yours. Be sure to keep the focus on the questions that students formulate, and remind students that they are free to ask questions without judgment.

→ Although the tool highlights three distinct phases (observe, describe, question), the truth is that observations and questions sometimes occur simultaneously. Allow students to record questions as they occur, but don't encourage the conflation of observation and question generating, as the larger goal is to give students focused time for careful observation before generating questions.

→ During the sharing of student questions, you may want to guide the discussion to help students generate a larger pool of questions. Use language like this to elicit more questions:

- Can anyone generate a question about something that you observed but that we don't yet have a question about?

- These are all great questions. But can you see how they can all be answered with one or two words? Let's try to get some questions that would require more developed responses. How about some *why* and *how* questions? Can we come up with some of those?

- What about the advantages and disadvantages that having quills might pose for the porcupine? Can anyone come up with any questions about advantages or disadvantages?

- Now let's really challenge ourselves and go for some truly "outside the box" questions. See if you can generate a question that's totally unique and creative. Any takers?

→ Prepare students for success by modeling the different kinds of questions that they can ask. Help them see the difference between closed-ended questions that can be answered with a *yes, no,* or a single word/phrase versus open-ended questions that require explanation or elaboration. Encourage them to generate different kinds of questions by familiarizing them with the four question types described below and the associated "starter words": *who, what, when, where, why, how,* and *what if.* Note that the sample questions for each question type are taken directly from the classroom lessons in Examples 1, 2, and 3.

- *Who, what, when,* and *where* questions ask for specific information. For example, "Who makes decisions about things like temperature?" or "What determines where a customer gets seated?"

- *How* questions ask for explanations of processes or phenomena. For example, "How do fish breathe?" or "How does the restaurant determine how much food to buy (risk of running out vs. spoiling)?"

- *Why* questions ask for causes or reasons. For example, "Why does one fish swim more?" or "Why did the author use such 'cool' language to describe such a gruesome crime scene?"

- *What if* questions ask for speculation. For example, "What if large groups were seated at round tables instead?"

The Write Way to Motivate

What is it?

A tool that makes writing about classroom content motivating for students by replacing run-of-the-mill writing tasks with tasks that invite creativity, discovery, and personal expression

What are the benefits of using this tool?

Creative writing has long been used as a way to engage students' natural curiosity, as it allows students to play with ideas and express themselves in their own voices. But not all writing can be open-ended and exploratory. So how can we get students to pursue content-based writing with the same zeal as creative writing? By using this tool's seven writing frames, which invite students to view classroom content through thought-provoking lenses and express their ideas in interesting ways. Regular use of these frames can help turn student writing assignments from routine exercises into journeys of discovery and self-expression.

What are the basic steps?

1. Review the writing frames on pp. 89–90. Select a frame that you believe will develop students' understanding or appreciation of what they're learning.

Note: If multiple frames seem appropriate, you can pick more than one. Giving students a choice of frames to complete in Step 2, rather than requiring everyone to complete the same one, can be a real motivation booster!

2. Introduce and explain the selected frame(s) to students. Clarify the purpose of the assignment, type of thinking/writing that it requires, and the criteria you'll use to evaluate students' work.

3. Encourage students to have fun with the assignment. Emphasize that it's not only a chance to show what they know; it's also a chance to think and express themselves in creative and original ways.

4. Use students' completed pieces to assess their understanding of the content and their command of the requisite writing skills. Work with students as needed to address any gaps or deficiencies.

5. Help students reflect on the value of thinking and writing about content in new and unusual ways. Use questions like these to get the ball rolling: Did this assignment affect your motivation in any way? The amount you learned? Your appreciation of or attitude toward the material?

How is this tool used in the classroom?

✔ To get students excited about content-based writing

✔ To deepen learning by helping students think about content in new and unusual ways

✔ To help students gain comfort writing in different styles and for different purposes

Seven Motivating Writing Frames

Make It Amazing!

This frame challenges students to take something they're learning about and tell people why that something is amazing. The goal is to help students find the excitement in what they're learning—to get beyond textbook descriptions and discover aspects of the content that are especially noteworthy, impressive, or unusual. For example, a student who wants to "make dolphins amazing" might focus in on their uncanny problem-solving skills, best-in-nature echolocation (aka sonar), and the fact that they give themselves names through unique whistle signatures.

How the Heck Does It Work?

How does the human body convert food into energy? How does a high-volume restaurant create made-to-order meals for hundreds of people each night? How do horror writers make us sit on the edges of our seats using only words? The question of how things work—how they perform their functions or achieve their goals—can be highly intriguing. This frame puts the question of *how* directly to students, challenging them to figure out and explain how things we often take for granted actually work. A variation on this frame is How the Heck Did It Happen?, which asks students to examine a historical event or period and explore key factors that led to its occurrence.

Skeptikos

This frame, whose name comes from a Greek root meaning *inquiring*, encourages students to unleash their inner skeptic and question people's claims and interpretations rather than accepting those claims and interpretations as fact. (Students might, for example, investigate whether a politician's dubious-sounding claim is actually true—or whether a commonly accepted interpretation of a poem holds up under close scrutiny.) Once students complete their analyses, they should share their findings and present their evidence. ("I don't agree with the common interpretation that the narrator was satisfied with his choice because…") Encouraging students to question what they see and hear can be incredibly motivating and empowering; it also helps them develop the "questioning habit"—a habit of mind that's exhibited by good thinkers in all disciplines (Costa & Kallick, 2008).

A Day in the Life

A Day in the Life stimulates curiosity and creative thinking by inviting students to imagine what life would be like as a notable figure (e.g., a soldier awaiting the storming of Normandy), character (e.g., Matilda), or concept/object (e.g., van Gogh's paintbrush). Students then write about some aspect of their life (e.g., what they do, see, feel, think, wonder about) from the perspective of that object or individual. Depending on your goals, you can have students "write what they want" or give them a specific task. For example:

- Choose the biography from this unit that you identified with most. "Become" the person it was about, and reflect on the greatest challenge you ever faced. Write three diary entries that reveal what you faced, what you were thinking, and how you worked through the challenge.

- Imagine that you are a member of one of the endangered species we learned about. What is life like for you? What makes survival difficult? What do you wish you could tell people about your situation so that they might act to help your species survive?

Clarify that in all cases, students should use what they know about the relevant content to inform their writing, not just make things up out of thin air.

What You Think You Know Ain't Always So

When people learn that something they believe to be true isn't actually true, they're usually motivated to find out why. This tool aims to spark that same kind of motivation in students by presenting them with a common misconception (e.g., the misconception that it's rare for two students in a class to share the same birthday) and revealing that it's wrong. Students are then challenged to figure out and explain why. Exploring and taking apart misconceptions helps students develop an understanding of the relevant concepts and principles (e.g., principles of *probability* in the birthday example above). It also teaches them a broader lesson about the importance of checking one's assumptions by showing them that "what you think you know ain't always so!"

What If?

This frame uses "what if" questions like these to motivate creative and speculative thinking about classroom content:

- What if the United States had never entered World War II?

- What if Jonas refused to accept the role of the Giver?

- What if photosynthesis were reversed, so that plants consumed oxygen and created carbon dioxide?

- What if the sum of a triangle's angles didn't always equal 180 degrees? How would Euclidean theorems change as a result?

The idea is to see whether students can use what they've learned about a specific topic or text to predict the possible consequences of changing that topic or text in some way (e.g., changing a known fact, redefining a scientific principle, undoing an important action). When responding to the World War II question above, for example, students would be encouraged to use what they had learned about the impact of the United States entering World War II to imagine how the world might be different if the United States hadn't entered the war.

From Frightened to Enlightened

There is cathartic power in staring down a fear or challenge. From Frightened to Enlightened is a frame that encourages students to "jump into the deep end" by daring them to develop an appreciation for something that they tend to avoid, that makes them uncomfortable, or that they have prejudicial views about—and then share their enlightened views with others. A world studies teacher might help students move "from frightened to enlightened" regarding the dietary habits of other cultures by challenging them to make a case for why eating insects isn't a gross or crazy idea, but rather an idea that makes good sense. A music teacher might challenge students to convince themselves and others why a type of music they think they hate (e.g., opera) is really worthy of their admiration. The reward of this frame is significant, as it helps students fill in knowledge gaps ("I never knew that about opera!") and achieve the sense of pride that comes from overcoming fears and prejudices.

Epilogue: Looking Back to Go Forward

We've made the case for curiosity, outlined three key goals for promoting curiosity in every classroom (sparking curiosity, fanning the flame, and creating an inner fire), and provided tools you can use to achieve these goals. Now it's up to you to try the tools in your classroom, reflect on how well they work, and think about steps you can take to get them working even better.

The reflection form on the next page was designed to help you look back on your practice and use what you learn to establish concrete plans for improvement. We encourage you to use the form regularly and save your responses, along with copies of relevant artifacts (e.g., lesson plans, handouts, classroom posters, samples of student work). Creating this kind of "reflection journal" will enable you to look back on and learn from your experiences, document growth over time (yours and your students'), and share what you've been doing with colleagues and/or supervisors. A sample journal entry is shown below.

REFLECTING ON MY PRACTICE

1) What tool did I use? On what date? With what group of students or class?

   I used Claim Check with my entire class on September 15th.

2) Have I used this tool before? No.

3) How did I build the tool into my lesson plans? And for what purpose?

   With the presidential election coming up, and candidates' ads, claims, and tweets popping up everywhere, I felt like it was important to help my students learn to think critically about the things politicians say when they're trying to get elected. Claim Check seemed perfect for this purpose.

4) Did I use the tool as written or modify it in any way? (Explain any modifications.) I used it as written.

5) What worked well? What (if any) issues or challenges did I face?

   With regard to my overall goal, the tool worked great—finding that politicians' claims didn't always "check out" helped my students recognize the importance of being more critical consumers of information. But my students weren't able to work as independently as I had hoped. They needed help determining which sources were credible, how to handle contradictory information, etc.

6) What might I do differently the next time I use this tool to make it work even better?

   Before I use this tool again, I will explicitly teach and model the skills that are needed to check a claim successfully, as advised in Step 3 of the tool. I skipped this step because I thought my students would've already learned these skills, but it became clear that wasn't the case.

7) How did the tool affect me, my students, and/or our classroom environment?
   (Did it affect factors like engagement, effort, or collaboration? Did it promote better behavior, thinking, or learning? Did it enhance my teaching, my relationships with students, or the classroom environment?)

   My students were surprised to find that many claims don't check out, and that really motivated them to check and question the others. They got into this task way more than I thought they would!

8) Would I use this tool again and/or recommend it to a colleague? Why or why not?

   Yes. The tool develops valuable skills and habits of mind (being skeptical, evaluating claims, finding evidence)—and it does it in a way that students enjoy! It could be used in all content areas.

Reflecting On My Practice

1) What tool did I use? On what date? With what group of students or class?

2) Have I used this tool before?

3) How did I build the tool into my lesson plans? And for what purpose?

4) Did I use the tool as written or modify it in any way? (Explain any modifications.)

5) What worked well? What (if any) issues or challenges did I face?

6) What might I do differently the next time I use this tool to make it work even better?

7) How did the tool affect me, my students, and/or our classroom environment?

   (Did it affect factors like engagement, effort, or collaboration? Did it promote better behavior, thinking, or learning? Did it enhance my teaching, my relationships with students, or the classroom environment?)

8) Would I use this tool again and/or recommend it to a colleague? Why or why not?

References

Aron, A. R., Shohamy, D., Clark, J., Myers, C., Gluck, M. A., & Poldrack, R. A. (2004). Human midbrain sensitivity to cognitive feedback and uncertainty during classification learning. *Journal of Neurophysiology, 92*(2), 1144–1152.

Benedict, B. M. (2001). *Curiosity: A cultural history of early modern inquiry.* Chicago, IL: University of Chicago Press.

Boutz, A. L., Silver, H. F., Jackson, J. W., & Perini, M. J. (2012). *Tools for thoughtful assessment: Classroom-ready techniques for improving teaching and learning.* Ho-Ho-Kus, NJ: Thoughtful Education Press.

Brownlie, F., Close, S., & Wingren, L. (1990). *Tomorrow's classrooms today: Strategies for creating active readers, writers, and thinkers.* Portsmouth, NH: Heinemann.

Costa, A. L. (2008). *The school as a home for the mind: Creating mindful curriculum, instruction, and dialogue* (2nd ed.). Thousand Oaks, CA: Corwin Press.

Costa, A. L., & Kallick, B. (Eds.). (2008). *Learning and leading with Habits of Mind: 16 essential characteristics for success.* Alexandria, VA: ASCD.

Crowther, D. J., & Cannon, J. (2004). Strategy makeover: From "know," "want," "learned" to "think," "how," "conclude," a popular reading strategy gets a science makeover. *Science and Children, 42*(1), 42–44.

Dean, C. B., Hubbell, E. R., Pitler, H., & Stone, B. (2012). *Classroom instruction that works: Research-based strategies for increasing student achievement* (2nd ed.). Alexandria, VA: ASCD.

Duckworth, A. (2016). *Grit: The power of passion and perseverance.* New York, NY: Simon & Schuster.

Duffelmeyer, F. A. (1994). Effective anticipation guide statements for learning from expository prose. *Journal of Reading*, 37(6), 452-457.

Engel, S. (2011). Children's need to know: Curiosity in schools. *Harvard Educational Review, 81*(4), 625–645.

Engel, S. (2015). *The hungry mind: The origins of curiosity in childhood.* Cambridge, MA: Harvard University Press.

Engelhard, G., & Monsaas, J. A. (1988). Grade level, gender and school-related curiosity in urban elementary schools. *Journal of Educational Research, 82*(1), 22–26.

Fernández-Aráoz, C. (2014). 21st century talent spotting. *Harvard Business Review, 92*(6), 46–56. Retrieved from https://hbr.org/2014/06/21st-century-talent-spotting

Goodwin, B. (2018). *Out of curiosity: Restoring the power of hungry minds for better schools, workplaces, and lives.* Denver, CO: McREL International.

Goodwin, B., Gibson, T., Lewis, D., & Rouleau, K. (2018). *Unstuck: How curiosity, peer coaching, and teaming can change your school.* Alexandria, VA: ASCD.

Goodwin, B., Rouleau, K., & Lewis, D. (2018). *Curiosity works: A guidebook for moving your school from improvement to innovation.* Denver, CO: McREL International.

Gordon, W. J. J. (1973). *The metaphorical way of learning and knowing.* Cambridge, MA: Porpoise Books.

Gottfried, A. E., Fleming, J., & Gottfried, A. W. (2001). Continuity of academic intrinsic motivation from childhood through late adolescence: A longitudinal study. *Journal of Educational Psychology, 93*(1) 3–13.

Gruber, M. J., Gelman, B. D., & Ranganath, C. (2014). States of curiosity modulate hippocampus-dependent learning via the dopaminergic circuit. *Neuron, 84*(2), 486–496.

Herber, H. (1970). *Teaching reading in the content areas.* Englewood Cliffs, NJ: Prentice Hall.

Kashdan, T. B., & Silvia, P. J. (2009). Curiosity and interest: The benefits of thriving on novelty and challenge. In C.

R. Snyder and Shane J. Lopez (Eds.), *Oxford handbook of positive psychology* (2nd ed.). New York, NY: Oxford University Press.

Kashdan, L., & Steger, M. (2007). Curiosity and pathways to well-being and meaning in life: Traits, states, and everyday behaviors. *Motivation and Emotion, 31*(3), 159–173.

Loewenstein, G. (1994). The psychology of curiosity: A review and reinterpretation. *Psychology Bulletin, 116*(1), 75–98.

Lowry, N., & Johnson, D. W. (1981). Effects of controversy on epistemic curiosity, achievement, and attitudes. *The Journal of Social Psychology, 115*(1), 31–43.

McTighe, J., & Silver, H. F. (2020). *Teaching for deeper learning: Tools to engage students in meaning making.* Alexandria, VA: ASCD.

McTighe, J., & Willis, J. (2019). *Upgrade your teaching: Understanding by Design meets neuroscience.* Alexandria, VA: ASCD.

Ogle, D. (1986). K-W-L: A teaching model that develops active reading of expository text. *The Reading Teacher, 39,* 564–570.

Reio, T. G., & Wiswell, A. (2000). Field investigation of the relationship among adult curiosity, workplace learning, and job performance. *Human Resource Development Quarterly, 11*(1), 5–30.

Roosevelt, E. (n.d.). *Eleanor Roosevelt quotes.* Retrieved from https://www.brainyquote.com/quotes/eleanor _roosevelt_161633

Rothstein, D., & Santana, L. (2011). *Make just one change: Teach students to ask their own questions.* Cambridge, MA: Harvard Education Press.

Rowe, M. B. (1972, April). *Wait-time and rewards as instructional variables: Their influence on language, logic, and fate control.* Paper presented at 1972 National Association for Research in Science Teaching conference, Chicago, IL.

Shah, P. (2018). Commentary on Shah, Weeks, Richards, & Kaciroti research findings. In B. Mostafavi. Exploring the link between childhood curiosity and school achievement, *University of Michigan Health Lab Blog.* Retrieved from https://labblog.uofmhealth.org/lab-report/exploring-link-between-childhood-curiosity-and -school-achievement

Shah, P. E., Weeks, H. M., Richards, B., & Kaciroti, N. (2018). Early childhood curiosity and kindergarten reading and math academic achievement. *Pediatric Research, 84*(3) 380–386.

Silver, H. F., Abla, C., Boutz, A. L., & Perini, M. J. (2018). *Tools for classroom instruction that works: Ready-to-use techniques for increasing student achievement.* Franklin Lakes, NJ: Thoughtful Education Press.

Silver, H. F., & Boutz, A. L. (2015). *Tools for conquering the Common Core: Classroom-ready techniques for targeting the ELA/literacy standards.* Franklin Lakes, NJ: Thoughtful Education Press.

Silver, H. F., Brunsting, J. R., Walsh, T., and Thomas, E. J. (2012). *Math tools, grades 3–12: 60+ ways to build mathematical practices, differentiate instruction, and increase student engagement* (2nd ed.). Thousand Oaks, CA: Corwin Press.

Silver, H. F., & Perini, M. J. (2010). The eight Cs of engagement: How learning styles and instructional design increase student commitment to learning. In R. J. Marzano (Ed.), *On excellence in teaching* (pp. 319–342). Bloomington, IN: Solution Tree Press.

Silver, H. F., Perini, M. J., & Boutz, A. L. (2016). *Tools for a successful school year (starting on day one): Classroom-ready techniques for building the four cornerstones of an effective classroom.* Franklin Lakes, NJ: Thoughtful Education Press.

Silver, H. F., Strong, R. W., & Perini, M. J. (2001). *Tools for promoting active, in-depth learning* (2nd ed.). Ho-Ho-Kus, NJ: Thoughtful Education Press.

Springsteen, B. (1998). *Songs.* New York, NY: HarperEntertainment.

Suchman, J. R. (1966). *Developing inquiry.* Chicago, IL: Science Research Associates.

Swan, G. E., & Carmelli, D. (1996). Curiosity and mortality in aging adults: A 5-year follow-up of the western collaborative group study. *Psychology and Aging, 11*(3), 449–453.

Taba, H., Durkin, M. C., Fraenkel, J. R., & McNaughton, A. H. (1971). *Teacher's handbook to elementary social studies: An inductive approach.* Reading, MA: Addison-Wesley.

Tobin, K. (1987). The role of wait time in higher cognitive level learning. *Review of Educational Research, 57*(1), 69–95.

von Stumm, S., Hell, B., & Chamorro-Premuzic, T. (2011). The hungry mind: Intellectual curiosity is the third pillar of academic performance. *Perspectives on Psychological Science, 6*(6), 574–588.

Wiggins, G., & McTighe, J. (2012). *The Understanding by Design guide to advanced concepts in designing and reviewing units.* Alexandria, VA: ASCD.

Index of Tools

About the Authors

Bryan Goodwin, MA, is the president and CEO of McREL International, a nonprofit organization that helps school systems worldwide improve student outcomes. He has spoken and delivered workshops to audiences worldwide and written several books, including *Out of Curiosity: Restoring the Power of Hungry Minds for Better Schools, Workplaces, and Lives*; *Curiosity Works: A Guidebook for Moving Your School from Improvement to Innovation*; *Unstuck: How Curiosity, Peer Coaching, and Teaming Can Change Your School*; *Balanced Leadership for Powerful Learning: Tools for Achieving Success in Your School*; *The 12 Touchstones of Good Teaching: A Checklist for Staying Focused Every Day*; and *Simply Better: Doing What Matters Most to Change the Odds for Student Success.* Bryan also writes a regular research column for ASCD's *Educational Leadership* magazine.

Harvey F. Silver, EdD, is the co-founder and president of Silver Strong & Associates and Thoughtful Education Press. A dynamic speaker and a leading expert on the use of practical, research-based techniques for improving classroom instruction, Harvey presents regularly at national and regional education conferences. He also works directly with schools, districts, and education organizations around the world, conducting workshops on a wide range of topics, including student engagement, differentiated instruction, thoughtful assessment, instructional leadership, and strategic lesson/unit design. He is the co-author of several education bestsellers, including *Tools for Classroom Instruction That Works*, *Tools for a Successful School Year*, *The Strategic Teacher*, and *The Core Six*. Harvey's newest publication is *Teaching for Deeper Learning*, a collaboration with fellow education thought leader, Jay McTighe.

Susan Kreisman, MS, a senior associate at Silver Strong & Associates, is an experienced educator, administrator, and coach. Susan was the co-founder and first principal of Manhattan Hunter Science High School in New York City, an early-college high school for diverse students that reports a 100 percent college admission rate. Previously, Susan served as an assistant high school principal and classroom English/reading teacher. She has also taught graduate-level courses in curriculum theory and development at the City University of New York. Susan works extensively with public and charter schools that commit to a "whole child" approach to education. As part of her work with school communities, Susan specializes in differentiated instruction, school leadership, educator effectiveness, and the development of professional learning communities.

Matthew J. Perini, MA, serves as the senior director of content development for Silver Strong & Associates and oversees all aspects of content development, including publishing, training designs, customized curriculum development, and content-based marketing. Matthew is the co-founder of Thoughtful Education Press (the publishing division of Silver Strong & Associates). Under Matthew's leadership and editorial direction, Thoughtful Education Press has become well known for its practical publications that provide educators with tools and strategies they can put to use immediately. Matthew is the series editor and a contributing author for Thoughtful Education Press's most prominent line of books, the award-winning Tools for Today's Educators series.

Notes

Notes

Notes

Notes